D0942900

PRAISE FOR KATE BIRDSALL

"Kate Birdsall's journey toward 'rightness' is a series of love stories, as Kate gradually comes to trust her love for the person she is. I admire Kate for the way she holds complexity, without needing to demonize parts of her past or paths not taken. This is a story of her transition, but it is more. It is a story of how love moves within us and, sometimes surprises, by moving us toward hope."

— Bill Sinkford, Senior Minister, First Unitarian Church, Portland

"With the increase in transgender visibility today, it's common to hear people ask, 'Where have all these trans people come from?' Kate Birdsall's elegant memoir demonstrates we've been here all along, we were just unable to live as our true selves. With honesty and wit, she shares the story of a life that, while rich and eventful, only came into focus at an age when the lives of many begin winding down. If you'd like to know more about the life of trans elders, this book is an excellent place to start."

— Mikki Gillette, staff member at Basic Rights Oregon

"*In Between*, the story of Kate Birdsall's youth and coming of age in the 1940s and 50s, before the adjective 'transgender' came into existence, is so compelling that it qualifies as a page-turner. The tensile strength of the writing, and a story that needs to be told more widely, show what it takes to come to an understanding of who one feels born to be. A great sense of peace develops as the book comes to a close, not only in the writer but in the reader. Who doesn't want to feel that they've grown into their most authentic self? I believe this book will save lives in a way that only 'story' can."

— Melissa Madenski, essayist, poet, and author of *Endurance*

"Kate's story is powerful and uplifting.... What a gift, to open the door to her experience with such clarity and self-awareness."

— Vassar Byrd, CEO Rose Villa Senior Living, Inc.

"Your story has helped me understand so many things that I have been thinking about. It's an amazing story. Every word is meaningful, clear, and heart-felt. It is such a journey toward healing and wholeness. I know that your experience will be an encouragement to [our grandchild] on their journey."

— Caroline, a friend whose grandchild is *In Between*

IN BETWEEN

A MEMOIR

KATE BIRDSALL

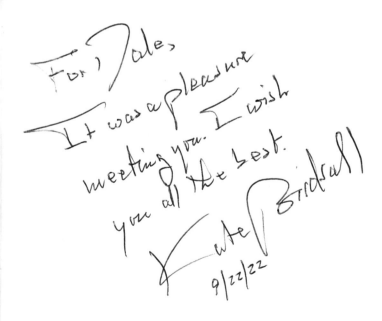

For Dale,
It was a pleasure
meeting you. I wish
you all the best.
Kate Birdsall
9/22/22

Copyright © Katherine D. Birdsall, 2021

All rights reserved. No part of this book may be reproduced or used in any manner without the prior written permission of the copyright owner, except for the use of brief quotations in a book review.

Disclaimer: These are my memories, from my perspective, and I have tried to represent events as faithfully as possible.

Cover design: Ruth Ross

CONTENTS

For Casey,
with love

1

OPENING ✳ 2011

"I believe that telling our stories, first to ourselves and then to one another and the world, is a revolutionary act."
— Janet Mock, *Redefining Realness*

I stood at the corner of 11th and Glisan, waiting for the streetcar. It was a glorious summer day in Portland, and I was thoroughly enjoying my new city, my new-found freedom, and my even newer-found anonymity, when the homeless man sharing the streetcar stop with me asked, "Are you transgender?"

It is such an odd question – potentially embarrassing if I wasn't transgender or, equally, if I was. This was the first time anyone had ever asked me that. I knew that some people knew I was transgender and others did not know, but for the vast majority, I had no idea. They treated me as they found me: an older woman, happy to be alive.

I had moved to Portland from a much smaller place, where it seemed at least half the town already knew I was transgender. I'd thought I'd been prepared for that question, answering with surprise, "Now why would you ask that?" which would throw it back to the questioner and perhaps satisfy my own curiosity as to what it was that made them question me. But when the question finally did come up, I just replied simply, as if he'd asked if I was right-handed, "Yes, I am." The homeless man, his curiosity satisfied, turned away to look for the streetcar.

Although we would like to be heroes in our own stories, some of us don't manage that. Maybe we just want to get by, without stirring things up. Even so, events don't always allow that.

In third grade, along with everyone else in my class, I had to fill out some kind of form. I don't remember what it was for, but I do remember one question: Religion. It was multiple-choice, leaving no room for creativity. The choices were: Protestant, Catholic, Jewish, Other. In that order. I was Unitarian. I didn't think I fit into any of the first three categories, so I checked Other. I didn't particularly want to be Other. In fact much of my life I've tried hard not to be Other, but it seemed too often that none of the choices fit and I was left as an Other.

I was born 20 years before the word transgender was coined. I was in college when the word first appeared in the scientific literature, but by then my Psych 101 teacher had killed whatever tepid interest I had in studying psychology. And I was more interested in objects, not beings. Objects were better defined, with edges. I had enough trouble defining myself without making a career of thinking about poorly-defined feelings and actions and interactions.

Forty years later I know I am transgender, but living in a new place where no one knew me, I was delighted to pretend that I'm not. I'd told my doctor, of course, but not my dentist or hairdresser or neighbors or new friends. If they knew without my telling, that was fine, but I wasn't going to bring it up.

Well, actually, there was more to it than that. I avoided the fact of my being transgender. When I told a little of my history – where

I'd lived, that I'd been married, where I'd worked – I used gender-neutral words and edited as I went. The stories became more difficult the deeper they went. It took me awhile to realize that I'd built myself another box to live in and needed to free myself from that one, too. It'd taken me much too long to free myself from the first one. To even recognize the box.

2

HOPING ✳ 1943-1957

"Listen to the mustn'ts, child. Listen to the don'ts. Listen to the should-n'ts, the impossibles, the won'ts. Listen to the never haves, then listen close to me... Anything can happen, child. Anything can be."
— Shel Silverstein

I don't remember her name. She lived in the yellow brick house across the street – the one with the bus driver. It was a typical summer day in Detroit – hot and sticky, with not a hint of breeze to stir the thick air. We were in my backyard. The lawn was a deep, rich green; the quince tree and the bushes along the fence and garage were full and lush.

I don't remember how old we were, but we were young – very young – but we weren't toddlers anymore. We could run and jump and dance with joy. We were too young to have learned restraint or social norms – too young to be inhibited yet. We did what children that age do – play and laugh and explore and learn.

At some point in our play, we got too hot from the summer afternoon. Perhaps we knew enough not to get our clothes wet. We stripped them off before playing with the garden hose, squirting each other. It was fun, silly, with lots of laughter.

Our bodies were the same, but she had just a small cleft between her legs – almost like the drawings of cherubs that were popular at that time. The cherubs had shirts but no pants, with only smooth skin between their legs. Unlike me. I had a growth between my legs. It was a bit like those bumps on the tree that I had seen while walking with my father. He had explained that the growth on the tree didn't hurt it, but it was not really part of the tree. It was a foreign organism. What did he call it? A parasite? That's what I had between my legs.

I can see her body clearly, even now. It made quite an impression on me, this difference between us. It might be my earliest memory. For many years, my reaction to the body of the girl in the yellow brick house was not something I would tell anyone. I kept that part of me hidden, where it might be safe.

I had been born with a male body, so everyone assumed I was a boy. But sometime before going to kindergarten, I realized that something was wrong. I didn't doubt that I was male. I had a male body after all. But somehow I knew that I should be a girl, that I'd be happier as a girl, and that I'd fit into the world better as a girl.

I suppose this realization was about the time I learned that girls and boys are treated differently. There are different expectations for boys and girls. People speak to boys and girls differently, or at least they certainly did then. Some of the distinctions were very subtle, but small children are good at sensing those subtleties. That's how we learn, when we are small.

And this was in the 1940s, when gender roles were more constrained than they are today.

As a boy, I couldn't have dolls, but I could have teddy bears. Teddy bears were acceptable, barely. I started with Teddy, an old, well-worn bear that had passed from my sister to my brother to me. Gradually, I accumulated an extended family – perhaps a village. Teddy was the old man. Fuzzy was petite and stylish in her pretty black and white. She was the smart one. Foogie and Goulash were twins – identical except for their coloring. They were mischievous and would get into trouble. The dogs – Murpy and Burpy and Gurpy – were another family, or perhaps cousins. The relationships were not that defined. And there were more bears.

When I was six or seven, my mother taught me how to use the sewing machine to make clothes for my bears, but I was never very good at it and soon lost interest. To me, it was about how the bears interacted. Besides, they had fur to cover them, although Teddy was getting pretty bald in places. And they had nothing between their legs to conceal.

I was content to play with my bears alone, but sometimes I would play with my friend Gretchen. Some of my bears would visit her dolls or her dolls would visit my bears. Our families of bears and dolls were always friendly and got along, just as our parents were with each other.

Mostly, I was OK being a boy – at least while I waited. I was admonished to be more of a boy: Don't sit like that; you sit like a girl. Don't walk like that; you walk like a girl. Don't act like that. So I worked on being a boy.

Fortunately, I was intrigued by cars, trucks, trains, bicycles, scooters, wagons, buggies – anything with wheels. I wanted to know how they worked. I could see how a bicycle worked, but what about cars and trucks and trains? You pour gasoline or diesel in, or you build steam with coal or wood, and it made the machine move and work. And there were water wheels and windmills and mills powered by horses. Even things without wheels. How did a clock work? How did a telephone work? Perhaps my questions wouldn't have been answered as readily if they didn't think I was a boy. Gradually, I learned how machines worked.

But I didn't know how bodies worked. I remember a time

when I would be hopeful each night when I went to bed. Before falling asleep I would think: "Perhaps tonight will be the night when this extra stuff falls off – like how a scab falls off when the skin underneath heals. Then people would see that I'm a girl." I just thought my body would heal itself.

I never spoke of it. This was the 1940s – a time when people didn't talk about their bodies. And my family certainly didn't.

My neighborhood, like much of Detroit, was on a regular grid of straight streets intersecting at right angles. Our house, brick and blocky, was with similar brick and blocky houses, no two exactly alike. Large elm trees shaded the street. Every house had a front yard and a backyard. Some houses had driveways from the street to a garage on the back property line, but many were set too close together to allow for a driveway. Ours was one of those, snuggled close to the house next door. Beyond the back fence was a rough-paved alley. My father could put the car in the garage from there, our trash cans were there, and sometimes I would see an old man there, pushing his two-wheeled cart made from an old horse-drawn wagon, looking for bits of trash he could sell.

My grandparents lived down the street in their own blocky house – the one my father and his brother had grown up in. At the end of the block was Third Street, where my father would catch the bus to his office downtown.

My mother stayed home, cooking and cleaning and taking care of us kids. She was always active – League of Women Voters, Women's Alliance at the church, forming a neighborhood association to ease the transition to a mixed-race neighborhood. Elderly Mrs. Matthews would come once a week to help with the housework. She taught me how to tie my shoes.

My mother believed we kids should learn to take care of ourselves. We had chores – take out the trash, wash the dishes, clean our rooms, pick up the dog's droppings in the backyard. She also taught each of us basic cooking skills and how to do the laundry – things anyone should know in order to take care of themselves. It wasn't gender-based – my sister and brother and I had similar chores and learned the same things, although I don't remember my sister ever mowing the lawn.

Three blocks north on Third Street was my grade school, also brick and blocky. It was the same one my father and his brother had walked to, the one my sister and brother went to before me.

A mile south on Third was the General Motors Building, with three large showrooms filled with their latest offerings. It was an easy walk through the neighborhoods. A family story is that one day when I was three, my mother couldn't find me. She finally caught up to my brother and me several blocks down Third. We were walking to the General Motors Building to look at the cars. As the story goes, she took me home but let my six year-old brother proceed. It would be hard to get lost in the regular grid of the streets and he knew how to cross streets safely.

Across Third was a small park that took up the whole block. In the middle of the park was a small, open pavilion. My mother told me there used to be band concerts there in the summer. By the time I left high school, the city had removed the top of the pavilion so that miscreants couldn't hide there. But when I was young, we were still pretending we lived in a perfect world and the no-goodniks were somewhere else.

And it was a perfect world – safe, friendly, easy, confining, with rigid roles. Everyone knew where they fit into it. Well, almost everyone.

Every morning, Monday through Friday, my father would catch the bus to work. Every Sunday morning, we five would get in the car and go to the Unitarian-Universalist church. We'd get there early because both of my parents sang in the choir. And we'd stay late so they could socialize and do some committee work.

In the summer, my father took his vacation. We'd load up the car and go tent camping, increasing the range of our explorations as my father earned longer vacations. We were a happy family, quiet, respectful of each other. I wouldn't say we were close, though, or protective of each other. We kids were given the foundation from which to make our way in the world, and I'm thankful for that. It just took me awhile to find my way.

I was a boy, but I had trouble fitting into that role. I never liked the rough and tumble play many boys love. I only played with the neighborhood boys a few times. I didn't seek them out, and after a few attempts, they didn't try to include me.

There were a few vacant lots in my neighborhood, left when housebuilding stopped during the Depression. One lot was a few blocks up Third. It was much larger than most and covered the whole end of the block. It was filled with the tall trees and thick bushes that had grown naturally on this land before the city crept past it. There was a path worn diagonally across the lot, from people cutting the corner, but the lush vegetation could make it dark inside, and I usually avoided it. Toward the middle was a small clearing and a depression in the dirt. It looked like it might have been used as a small campground by men looking for work during the Depression, shielded from the street by the undergrowth, but in the post-war boom there was no longer a need to camp inside the city.

One day when I was seven or eight, I got swept up into a group of neighborhood boys. They had heard that some boys from the neighborhood on the other side of this large vacant lot had built a circle of stones and downed branches to form a low fort wall in the clearing. There was a lot of excited talk about taking the fort from them. We ran up the street, shouting as we went. It was all very exciting until we entered the woods.

There were maybe eight or ten of us now. I wasn't the smallest, but most were bigger and older. We gathered at the edge of the dry, dusty woods and crept up the path until we could see the boys in the fort. Then we rushed at them, hollering. There was no plan

– we just ran at them and began pushing, trying to shove them out of the fort. I put all I could into it but was no match for the larger, tougher boys. I was pushed down and fell awkwardly onto the branches and stones of the fort wall. Another boy fell on top of me.

Before long, all of the boys were inside the circle, and things began settling down. The angry shouts turned to loud, happy talk. The pushing and shoving turned to backslapping and congratulations. I didn't understand what had just happened. I was scratched and bruised from my fall but now we were all friends. Or they were all friends. It was as if I'd fallen among aliens, and I was an outsider once again. Bewildered, I slipped away. It was one of the few times I played with a group of boys.

Usually, I just played with Leon, who lived in the brown brick house across the street. We'd create roads and dig tunnels in a mud pile in his backyard, or we'd ride our bicycles along the sidewalks in front of his house.

Or I'd entertain myself alone, setting up a small town of paper houses in the back of my living room, where I'd be out of the way, running toy cars up and down the tiny streets. I knew some boys liked to crash their cars together, creating mayhem. But I didn't like mayhem. There seemed to be enough mayhem already in my quiet, regular, protected world.

In second grade I began helping my brother with his paper route. He delivered the afternoon paper – The Detroit News – in our neighborhood. His route was three blocks of our street and the two streets north of us. Most afternoons I would walk with him and run the papers up to the porches he indicated. Gradually, I learned the route and would do one side of the street while he did the other. He taught me to fold the papers so I could throw them and save steps and time. But if the paper didn't make it onto the porch, I would still have to run to get it and try again. With practice I managed to get it on the porch most of the time.

There were some customers who had special instructions, though – put the newspaper under the mat or put it inside the storm door.

After a year of helping my brother, he sold me the part of the route on our street, sold the other part to another boy, and bought a shorter route that had more customers because it was mostly apartments. (He found that was even more work, though, because with them he'd have to go inside each building and run up and down the hallway on each floor.) So at the age of eight, I had my own paper route. I felt very responsible but not particularly grown up.

We got our papers at an old wooden, two-car garage the News rented some blocks from our house. We paperboys – there were never girls – would gather at the garage after school or early in the morning on Sunday. The truck would arrive, the bundles were unloaded, and we would line up to get our allotted number of papers, fold some of them for throwing, stuff them into bags, and leave. Once the truck arrived, it was all very business-like, with some talking or calling back and forth, but each of us was eager to get our papers and leave.

Before the truck arrived was a different story, though. On normal days, there would be some horseplay. When the truck was late, things could get rowdy. Some boys would pitch pennies at one end of the garage. It is a betting game, where each player takes a turn tossing a coin toward the wall. The person who tossed the one closest to the wall won all the other coins. As it progressed, it could degenerate from fun to anger. I never participated. I was too cheap and, besides, at that age I never had any money with me. And anger scared me.

But there was other horseplay, too. Sometimes some shoving around, but I don't remember any actual fights. There was one time that for some reason a boy pulled his penis out of his pants and began twirling it around, chasing the other boys. It was the longest penis I've ever seen – perhaps that's what had precipitated the display.

I was the youngest and smallest boy at the paper garage, which offered me some protection. And my brother was there, at least for the first few years. He was Big Birdseed and I was Little Birdseed. The other boys recognized me as too young to participate in the rougher play.

After I'd been delivering papers for a few years, the man in charge of the garage told me that legally I had to be thirteen to work there. So if a lady in a black car asked me how old I was, I should say I was thirteen. That was OK with me, but I didn't know how well it would work. I always looked young for my age, and claiming to be thirteen when I was nine didn't sound like it would be convincing. Actually, I quit delivering papers when I was thirteen. At fourteen I started at a high school that was four miles away and wouldn't be able to get home and to the paper garage in time. Plus, after delivering papers every day for more than five years in rain and snow, sticky heat and winter darkness, I was ready to do something else. But the paper route had been an education. Delivering papers was a lesson in responsibility and constancy. Not getting caught up in the rougher horseplay at the garage was a lesson in keeping my head down, avoiding trouble, and getting by.

During my paper carrier time I became friends with Albert. We were the same age – nine or ten, probably. He lived in a brown brick house on the other end of the next block, in a different school district. I passed his house every day on my way to the newspaper garage and on the way home. He lived alone with his mother. I never asked about his father. One day while at his house, we were playing in the basement. He rooted through the laundry basket and put a slip and dress of his mother's over his clothes. He encouraged me to join in, but I was reluctant. I wasn't reluctant to dress up, but these were his mother's clothes, not his or mine. He assured me that his mother knew about him doing this and didn't mind.

I don't remember how often we did this. We'd dress in his mother's dirty laundry and play house in the unfinished basement, sitting on small chairs between the washing machine and the coal bin that wasn't used anymore, on the concrete floor under the clothes lines hanging from the wooden beams holding up the first floor. We would argue about who got to play the wife and who had to be the husband, unaware of any deeper meaning. Mostly we'd play the only roles we knew – husband and wife, with the wife cooking and taking care of the house, and the husband eating with her before kissing her good-bye and going off to work.

I never mentioned our play to anyone else. My parents let me do pretty much as I wanted. We would have to be home by the time the streetlights came on, or my mother would stand on the front porch and blow a horn made from a cow's horn. BA-WOOOOP! We could hear the sound on the next block. We were expected to look after ourselves and come home for meals or let her know if we were eating at a friend's house.

Albert's house was on the corner next to Hamilton Street. Our dress-up play lasted only one year. At the end of the school year his house and the next one would be taken down to make way for the John C. Lodge Expressway. I don't know where Albert and his mother moved, but one day after their house was empty he and I met there and, feeling very sinful, bashed holes in the walls. The house was about to be torn down, and we knew they wouldn't have been able to salvage the plaster walls anyway. Still, to me it seemed wrong for us to do this.

With Albert and his basement gone, I began to sneak into my sister's room from time to time and try on some of her things. She was in high school, six years older, and had developed what I thought of as a woman's body. Although I was ashamed of using clothes that weren't mine, I wasn't ashamed of putting on women's clothes.

I would go through her dresser drawers carefully, trying not to disturb anything. I was afraid of being caught. What I feared was confrontation for sneaking into my sister's room and being the cause of disappointment, confusion, and disruption for wearing her clothes.

I suppose Albert was a bad influence on me – one of a long string of friends like that through the years. But then, I might never have learned adventure without those bad influences. I was a shy child, even timid – a bit overwhelmed by life. I enjoyed my family excursions and playing by myself or with Leon, who lived across the street, or those times with Albert, or with Gretchen and her dolls. I was just trying to get by, trying to stay away from the large clot of tougher kids who lived down the street, or the ruffians in the park.

But mostly I was just a boy. I resented the freedom of girls to dress as they wanted, or the freedom it seemed they had. The grass is always greener, as the saying goes. Girls could wear pants and skirts, but I could wear only pants. Girls could have short or long hair, but my hair had to be short. Girls could play with dolls and giggle together or just be quiet. I was becoming aware of the social constraints women lived under, but my understanding was incomplete. And while I knew children grew and became adults, I couldn't quite associate how girls behaved with how I thought women had to be. And, being seen as a boy, I didn't receive the cultural messages that were part of the air that girls breathed.

One day when I was about eight or nine, I noticed a red dot on my scrotum. It appeared out of nowhere and was unlike anything else on me. Perhaps it was something that would grow to rot my boy parts off me! Could this be it? I tried not to be too hopeful, but it was odd. I even had my parents look at it. They didn't know what it was either, but they didn't think it was anything to worry about.

They didn't sense my hope. But it was not to be, because soon I had the dots on other parts of me and then we knew I had chicken pox.

I was nine in December, 1952, when news broke of Christine Jorgensen getting a sex change in Denmark. It was amazing, astounding, and oh so very strange. She was a freak, well outside our understanding of what it was to be human. I don't remember that my parents talked about her, but I read the newspapers I delivered. Her story made the front page. The Detroit News was a mainstream newspaper, not given to sensationalism, but I could read between the lines. This thing that Jorgensen did was incomprehensible. I didn't associate my feelings with her story. I wasn't odd. I wasn't a freak. I was just a boy who would be happier as a girl. The term "sex change" had no meaning that I understood. She was a man who became a woman. I was neither. Perhaps if she'd been a boy who became a girl I would have understood.

Looking back at it now, I sometimes wonder why I never talked about all this then. Part of it was that in my little slice of 1940s America, we didn't talk about our bodies, and certainly not our genitals. We didn't talk about our culturally-imposed roles. It didn't occur to us to talk about gender. Gender was a given. We didn't question it, Christine Jorgensen notwithstanding. Most people thought of gender and sex as the same thing, just that "gender" was a more polite way to say "sex." I didn't mention my feelings and my desires and my questioning and my incompletely-formulated ideas of being a girl because I didn't realize I had a choice.

I thought I should be a girl, but what would I say? Don't believe your eyes or the world, I'm really a girl despite all evidence to the contrary? I wasn't that strong. And who was I going to tell? Gretchen and I played together with our dolls as two children, almost un-gendered. Gretchen's mother, Carol, might have been sympathetic. My mother might, too, but she was a practical woman. Whether she was that way by nature or had been forced into it, I don't know. She loved me, I had no doubt, but she wanted me to be strong and independent. She had little time for romance or fantasy. I didn't want her to dismiss my feelings. I got enough of that from my older sister and brother and didn't need any more.

General Motors came out with the Corvette in 1953. It was small and so very appealing with its fiberglass body, invariably white, and with red seats in the small cockpit. I was only ten, but I really, really wanted one. For several years, a Corvette was the first item on my annual Christmas list. It was supplanted five years later by the Aston Martin DB4 – James Bond's car.

A Corvette was unattainable, beyond the realm of possibility. I was a kid, had no money and didn't know how to drive. But a Corvette existed; it was real. I could walk the mile down Third Street to the General Motors Building and sit in one, my left hand grasping the steering wheel, my right on the short, floor-mounted gearshift, dreaming. My being a girl was a dream, too, but it was in a whole different dimension, beyond the unattainable. The only way it could happen was to just happen.

Besides, the whole thing didn't make sense. Things were supposed to make sense. Everyone knew that fairy tales were just that – fairy tales. There was no fairy godmother who could make a pumpkin into a coach. There was no reason to believe I was anything other than a boy. It wasn't reasonable to think I could be a girl.

As puberty approached, I was still hopeful of being discovered to be a girl. In a way, I still believed in fairy tales. There was still a lot I didn't understand, and I could see no way to achieve girlhood. Being passive by nature, I resigned myself to my fate and hoped for the best. Yet for all that, I had been a happy child. But my age of innocence was waning, despite how I clung to it.

One evening I noticed that there was a hard spot about the size and shape of a Cheerio behind each of my nipples. This was it! I would grow breasts and then people would see that I was really a girl. But the hard spots didn't make my breasts grow. Before too many more months, the spots went away and I felt my body changing. I felt edgy, like something was taking me over – hormones, I know now. With these different feelings, I soon realized I was stuck being a boy and would grow to be a man, even though I had no idea how I would ever manage to be one.

3

COPING ✳ 1957-1961

"I guess in the end, it doesn't matter what we wanted. What matters is what we chose to do with the things we had."
— Mira Grant, *Deadline*

My grade school was just three blocks up Third Street, but junior high was a mile and half from our house. I could catch a city bus on the street by my grade school and, with my student pass, ride to junior high for a dime. And, if I could manage not to get robbed during the day, I could ride back home for another dime.

Durfee Junior High School sat on a large tract with two other schools – a grade school for that neighborhood and Central High School, the school grounds like a wart on the regular grid of streets. There were no main streets in front of the schools – access was through the neighborhoods, coarsened by the increased traffic. My own neighborhood was mixed racially and religiously, but it was solidly middle-class. Durfee gathered kids from a wider swath of the city. There were those of the mainstream and those outside that narrow channel.

After school was chaos, as kids poured out of the buildings. Some walked off toward their homes or a hangout, some formed groups on the school grounds, and some boarded the city buses that lined the curb, their route names above the front windows. Boarding the buses was never orderly, but in bad weather it was worse – the kids crowding the front doors, anxious to get on. Then there would be a struggle between the driver trying to close the doors and the kids trying to push on even though the bus was already packed solid.

When there was snow, some kids would throw snowballs at those crowding around the bus doors. Those in the back of the crowd would push forward even more, crushing those trying to step up into the bus. One time, as I sat on the bus a few rows behind the driver, a barrage of snowballs came deep into the bus, hitting those kids already on the steps, showering snow and ice on everyone in the front, including the driver. Fed up, he forced his way through the crowd and ran after those who had been throwing the snowballs. With no driver, kids rushed onto the bus, laughing because they wouldn't have to pay. Some emptied the coin changer by the fare box, and others stole his transfers. The driver returned, frustrated, to find he'd been robbed. Fuming and powerless, he closed the doors and drove us away. The kids laughed about how they had bested the driver, but I could only think of how he must feel and hoped he could get himself transferred to a route that didn't come by our school. I was beginning to understand that the world could be more harsh than the one I'd been living in.

Sometimes, to avoid the buses I walked home. Usually I walked through the neighborhoods and rarely encountered anyone, but one day I walked along the bus route. Close to my old grade school a group of larger boys came toward me down the sidewalk. I had a habit of looking down, trying to make my small self even smaller. No one had yet told me that I should make eye contact, although I doubt that I could have managed it even if I had heard the advice. Through experience I had learned that I was safer off in the corner, unnoticed or soon forgotten. Carrying my books and violin, I walked onto the grass next to the sidewalk, skirting the group of boys – my only acknowledgement of their presence – when, through my cloak of invisibility, came a fist, and then another.

I was on the ground, stunned by the violence and its suddenness. My eyes clouded with tears, I watched the boys walking away, going wherever they were going, as if nothing had happened. And for them, perhaps, nothing had.

I crawled around, shaking, gathering my books, checking to see if my violin was broken, very aware that cars continued passing on the street. No one checked to see if I was all right. Something had happened to me, but for the rest of the world nothing had happened, or at least nothing worth noticing.

After that I stayed out of arm's reach whenever possible. I continued to cling to my innocence, but it was getting more difficult.

I really disliked Durfee. It was a tough school, and I wasn't tough. I worried about going on to Central High next door, which I thought would be like Durfee but with older kids. My brother went to Cass Technical High School, a city-wide school with curriculum paths – Art, Music, Refrigeration and Air Conditioning, Home Ec, Chem-Bio, and more. My brother was in Auto-Aero. But entrance to Cass required good grades and an exam. I wasn't a good student, doing only enough to get by and happy with Cs and a sprinkling of Bs. My academic performance was based more on my feelings for the teacher than on the rigors of the class, but my teachers were uninspiring and I needed to be inspired to do more than the minimum. I didn't see how I could manage to get into Cass and worried that I'd be stuck going to Central. (It never occurred to me to work harder at Durfee so that I could go to

Cass. I still hadn't made the connection between effort and outcome.)

In the spring of my second year at Durfee, all eighth graders in the city took a standardized test. This was something new. There was going to be a new program at Cass Tech – an advanced program that would offer two years of math in one year and other accelerated classes – and those who scored in the top 2% on this test would be invited to go. I didn't think much about it.

About a month later, we received the results. With my score was a letter inviting me to attend the new Arts and Science Program at Cass Tech. I couldn't believe it. This was my way out of having to go to Central High. And not only that, the Cass program started in the ninth grade. I wouldn't have to go to Durfee next year!

I went home, thrilled that I might escape from Durfee and Central High. Amazed by my good fortune, I showed the letter to my mother. She read it several times and then, in disbelief, said: "And I always thought you were stupid." I replied: "I did too." We looked at each other, eyes wide with the wonder of it.

I survived my two years at Durfee. The door to my understanding of the world was still open only a crack, but I was starting to realize that many people live in a world much harsher than the one I knew.

Cass was a large school – seven stories high on the edge of downtown. It shared its facilities with the three-story High School of Commerce, which was connected to it by a bridge over the intervening street. On any school day, there were more than 10,000 students in the two buildings. I was confused and struggling and it would have been easy to get lost in the crush of students, but music gave me something to hang onto. Going through puberty was bad enough without at least having *something* to hang onto.

In junior high I'd played the violin in the orchestra. My brother played the baritone horn, and I liked its sound and had been learning to play it. Starting high school, I dropped the violin and joined the band, playing baritone horn. Instead of going to study hall, I worked in the music library with Gretchen and her friend Karen.

I learned to play both the trombone and tuba. Then the band director said I should learn bassoon since I had long fingers and some of the keys on a bassoon are a stretch to reach. It was my first reed instrument and I loved it.

As my male puberty progressed, the testosterone took me over and drove me in ways I found frightening. I didn't know who I was, and the testosterone didn't help. I still wanted to be a girl, but it felt like the testosterone had a mind of its own, pushing me in ways I didn't want and didn't understand. It was like in the movie "Invasion of the Bodysnatchers."

The testosterone wasn't the only problem, though. I could do the schoolwork in the advanced program, but I didn't fit in with the other kids. The advanced program was filled with overachievers, and at that point in my life I was a devoted underachiever. The advanced program was filled with kids you knew would go to a good college, get a good job, marry, and move to the suburbs where they would join a country club. The music program had a lot of misfits, and I gravitated to it. I was lost in high school, but music gave me a home, a base.

There were three bands at Cass, and I was playing a different instrument in each. When I was choosing my classes for the 11th grade, I wanted four music classes – three bands and a beginning class so I could learn string bass. My guidance counselor was exasperated with me. He threw up his hands and said, "You can't take that many out-of-curriculum classes. If you're going to do that, you might as well move to the music curriculum." He said it like it was a bad thing, a stupid idea. But I, being stubborn, said, "OK, I will."

So I transferred to the music curriculum. Then I could take all the music classes I wanted. A side benefit was that I got a new counselor.

At times I thought I was invisible, or at least wished I was. Often people seemed to ignore me, and there were plenty of times I preferred that. Not sure of who I was, I wanted to be just one of the crowd. Being singled out – for either something good or something bad – was painful. I had been physically attacked a few times, but I feared that less than derision, being made fun of. That and being shamed were my biggest fears. Thinking I should be a girl seemed natural to me, and I didn't think it was at all shameful. But I sensed that voicing that could open me up to what I dreaded most.

Through high school, I continued the surreptitious crossdressing I'd begun in fifth grade. I didn't have a complete outfit but that didn't matter to me. My sister was off to college, but I had a few things I'd either "borrowed" from her or had managed to acquire on my own. I did this in secret, afraid of being discovered. However, one day I went to school wearing an empty bra under my shirt. I thought no one could tell, and no one mentioned it, but thinking back I wonder if the outline showed across my back. I did it only that once, too afraid of being discovered to try again. Besides, it wasn't that satisfying. It had been exciting to think about ahead of time, but it had been an uneasy day. Hiding that I should be a girl was hard enough without spending the day hiding what I was wearing. I tended to stay in the background as much as I could so no one would notice I was odd, but wearing something under my clothes meant I had to hide even more. Whatever was driving me to wear girl's clothes didn't include publicly being a boy in girl's clothing. At least in private I could fantasize that I *was* a girl.

With all hope of being a girl lost, I needed to see if I could learn how to be a man. My father and his father were men, but they didn't do manly things. Both of them were civil engineers and worked in offices. They both were very handy and could fix all sorts of things. But neither liked sports or hunting or fishing. They loved the outdoors, but my juvenile mind in the 1950s equated manhood with toughness, sports, hunting and fishing. Gretchen's father Carl was an engineer, too. And Leon's father was a college professor. With no adequate manly role model, I muddled along. I didn't particularly want to be tough and had found I was too unco-ordinated for sports. The only part of hunting that sounded the least bit interesting to me was stomping around in the woods in the fall, but I'd read too many newspaper reports of hunters acci-dentally shooting each other. The north woods was the last place I wanted to be during hunting season. Carl had taken Gretchen and me fishing once. We sat on a dock on Lake Huron for several peaceful hours and each of us caught a fish. Carl cleaned and cooked the perch for us. I enjoyed the quiet time with Carl and Gretchen, and the fish were delicious. But afterwards, I figured: "OK, I've done that. I don't need to do it again." With all these good, smart, gentle men as models for me, I have no idea why I thought I had to be different. But I did. Perhaps it was the movies.

Or it could have been overcompensation. Through the years, I've seen people overshoot the mark in their attempt to be someone they aren't naturally. It wasn't denial, though – denial is the anti-LGBT Congressman caught soliciting sex in a men's room, or the trans-woman who was a brutal misogynist before accepting herself. I wasn't in denial, at least not yet. I was male and thought I should be a girl, but I was still male. I didn't think I *was* a girl – that was just something I had hoped for, like a Corvette or Aston Martin. My mother's practicality must have rubbed off on me at least a little, because I thought that I just had to figure out how to fit into society's expectations of me.

The suicide rate for trans youth is three times that for all youth. Puberty can be tough. Getting the wrong puberty can be even worse. And if you don't have people around you who understand, it can be devastating. I may have been saved by my passivity and ignorance. I had come to know that I couldn't be a girl, but I just saw the problem only as needing to adapt to the new reality. And somehow I knew that things could get better, even though I couldn't see how.

Again, what were the options? In the mid-1950s, the word transgender wouldn't exist for another ten years, and the first sex-change operation in the United States, performed with no publicity, was almost fifteen years away. The searchable internet was at least forty years in the future. It was the fairy godmother or nothing. I had no idea that options might even exist.

My high school friend was Gerry. He was a bit wild and got us into situations I never would have thought of. Sometimes we'd double date. He would usually fix me up with a friend of the girl he was interested in. He thought Catholic school girls were good dates because they would be looser than the girls we knew from public school. I don't know where he would meet these girls, and I can't attest to their morals or lack of them.

One night we went to a party in Ann Arbor. He was the only one there who I knew. I don't know what his connection to the host was, but that was Gerry. The party was at someone's house. The kids were about our age – high school seniors and college freshmen. I don't remember that there was any drinking. We just sat around talking and listening to music, some couples making out in the dark corners, some dancing. We were inside the house and in the back yard. It was dim and low-key.

At some point in the evening a girl announced that her cousin was visiting and had been taught how to read palms by a grandmother. Those nearby got excited, sensing something fun. The girl who knew how to read palms looked like us – nondescript middle-class white kids of the early 60s – but suddenly she seemed exotic. A bunch of us crowded around, asking for a reading. The girl read a few, pronouncing in mock seriousness that this person would have a long life and that one would travel. It was all very general, light-hearted and fun.

Gerry encouraged me to have her read my palm. Everyone was all smiles. The girl started out like with the others, but then she seemed startled. She kept looking at my palm and got very serious, almost disturbed. The air in the room changed. The palm reader, no longer having fun said, "I see a dark-haired woman on a hill. She keeps beckoning to you. You keep trying to climb the hill but you can't reach her no matter how hard you try. She's very sad and keeps beckoning to you."

The girl reading my palm looked badly shaken. She dropped my hand and rushed out of the room followed by her cousin. All the other kids stood around looking at each other wondering what had just happened. Gradually the party started up again.

Ordinarily, I would dismiss the reading as hokum, but the palm reader's reaction was so affecting I wondered if it actually had some meaning. At the time and for years afterward, when I thought of this girl's reading of my palm, I thought that I would be unlucky in love – that I would be drawn to a woman who wanted me but our getting together would be stymied through some failing of mine. Now, almost 60 years later, I wonder if she saw the woman I am who was buried so deeply within me.

Back in the real world, I still didn't know what I wanted to do with my life. I enjoyed playing in the bands, but it was just something I was doing in high school and knew I'd leave it behind. As graduation approached, I was adrift and becoming more and more lost. I thought perhaps I could go into the military for a tour to give myself a chance to grow up a little, but my parents wanted me to go to college. I think they were afraid that if I didn't go right after high school, I wouldn't go at all.

The only one in my family who had any military experience was my father's younger brother, John. He'd been in the Navy during World War II and, as a Spanish speaker, he had been assigned to a ship guarding the coast of South America from Nazi invasion. He'd found the duty tedious and boring and advised me to go to college, too.

This was 1961. Although the U.S. had already been involved with Vietnam for six years, there were only about 3,000 troops stationed there and the U.S. involvement wasn't on my mind. To me, it was the peacetime military that I wanted to join. All of us kids had been aware of possible nuclear attack since the "duck and cover" drills of elementary school in the early 1950s, but war on the ground wasn't in my thinking. I just wanted time away from school to experience life and maybe figure a few things out. The military sounded like a safe way to do that. But I wasn't strong enough to resist the pressure to continue my schooling.

My mother suggested that I go to Wayne State in Detroit, but I wanted to get away from home. There wasn't anything wrong with my home. I just wanted to strike out on my own a little but was too timid to just take off. I needed the structure of the military or college. I ended up applying for and barely being accepted to Antioch, a small, liberal-arts college in Ohio. My father and Uncle John had gone there. My sister had gone there. My brother and Gretchen were there then. It seemed a safe choice, and its co-op program, where we would alternate quarters at school with quarters working at a job the college found for us, sounded like it might help me figure out a way into my future.

I had no expectations. I figured I'd just keep going on whatever track I got pushed toward and I'd either figure it out or not. Eventually I'd get some job, marry, maybe have the average of 2.4 children, and live a normal, uneventful, dull life. I didn't think about it. I was just letting the fates push me wherever, with no ambition.

Upon graduation from high school, Gretchen's mother told

me: "Now you are a man." I just looked at her. I couldn't see how graduating high school made me a man. Besides, I didn't think that I would ever manage to become a man, regardless of how my body developed or whatever I might be able to accomplish. It just seemed like a bridge much, much too far.

4

SUPPRESSING ✳ 1961-1970

"She had been defeated by herself alone, and the sadness of it left a dark shadow in her heart. It further sapped her confidence and left her ever more withdrawn, ever more capable of suppressing her feelings. Like her roughened hands, her sensitivity was slowly being hardened, and she drew relief from the numbness creeping through her."
— Yo Yo, *Ghost Tide*

Entering Antioch, I had to pick a major and defaulted to Engineering. My father and Gretchen's father were engineers. I liked figuring out how machines and bridges and other physical things worked and had trouble figuring out how society and living organisms like people worked, so engineering sounded like as good a choice as any. Plus, that could set me up for some co-op jobs in the field, to see if I really wanted to be an engineer. It turned out that for me the jobs were the best part.

The college would find the jobs for us, but we were expected to get ourselves to wherever they were and find our own housing. My first jobs were male-oriented – surveyor's assistant, UPS garage janitor, messenger boy, construction site bookkeeper, plywood mill laborer. I usually liked the work, but I never quite fit in with the men. When I got an office job, I found I liked it and sought more. Office jobs were cleaner and usually temperature-controlled. I liked that there were pictures on the walls and a few well-behaved plants confined to their pots. Besides, I could wear nicer clothes and was less likely to hurt myself. I was good at organizing things, and that seemed to be a big part of office work. I loved sorting mail, filing, and typing drafts into polished letters. It seemed a natural fit.

The college itself offered me very little direction. It was geared toward self-directed people, and that wasn't me. I rattled around like a marble in an empty cigar box. I had never learned to study, and with no internal direction to my life, the loosely-structured academic program wasn't helpful.

I struggled with the challenges of the coursework and living with my dorm-mates and going off every three months to work at unfamiliar jobs in unfamiliar places. With these more immediate challenges, my gender issues receded into the background but in no way disappeared. I experimented a bit with my clothing, wearing women's pants and less masculine tops. This, of course, didn't help with my desire to fit in.

There were a few times when I would be in a group of students, the only boy among girls. We might be sitting around a table, talking, comfortable, enjoying our time together. At some point someone would realize that I was there, and the tone of the conversation would change. The girls would become a little guarded, having a boy in their midst. I hated when that happened but knew of no way around it.

I dated quite a bit in high school, double-dating with Gerry and getting dates on my own with girls I knew at school. I liked being among girls and I was sexually attracted to girls – two different urges I hadn't figured out how to blend together. But I dated very little in college. Instead of finding my way, I was becoming more lost.

I hit a wall in Calculus II, which was a required course for Engineering. After flunking it a second time, I was cast adrift. I tried several different majors but settled into Administration and Accounting, which I enjoyed, sort of, and didn't find too difficult.

We only went to school two quarters of the year and worked the other two quarters, with the result that the usual Antioch curriculum took five years to complete. There were a few who managed to do it in four, but very few. After I flunked Calc II and took too many introductory courses trying to find a major, it took me six years.

Toward the end, I was just marking time. Even though I lived in a dorm on campus, I had little social contact. I began sleeping twelve to fourteen hours a day. I was just going through the motions of being a student, of being alive. Even now, 50 years later, I will have a dream now and then where I wake up at Antioch and realize the final exam is that day. In the dream I realize I haven't been to any of the classes or read any of the books. I'm not even sure where I need to go to take the exam.

I felt stuck in a maze. I had no direction, no ambition. I was going with the flow. I wasn't trying to swim in any particular direction. I was too busy trying to keep my head above the water.

I held onto the idea of the military giving me some direction. Being in southwestern Ohio, near the Wright Brothers' home and Wright Patterson Air Force Base, I went to an Air Force recruiter. He was interested. I took a bunch of tests and did very well, especially on the navigator portion. But he wanted me to get my degree so that I could go to officer training. Being a navigator sounded interesting to me, but then I found out it was also the bombardier. I might have trouble with that aspect, but I was good at not worrying about things until I had to and put it out of my mind.

The war in Vietnam was heating up and much in the news. I

remember some guys talking about the jobs or the kind of work they were going to do after graduation. Having those kinds of plans seemed silly to me – of course we were all going to get swept up as cannon fodder in the war.

Jim, my roommate before he married, went on to grad school and kept his student deferment. He was studying for his PhD in research chemistry, so he also had a national security deferment. I was a poor student and barely made it to graduation. I wouldn't be accepted by any grad school, and I had no idea what field I would pursue anyway. My degree was in Administration – not exactly conducive to getting a national security deferment. I was resigned to being drafted.

I considered fleeing to Canada to avoid the draft. I liked Canada, but I had no connections there and didn't know how I would live. And word was that I'd never be able to return to the US, even for a visit. I wasn't ready to exile myself in that way.

I also thought of faking something that would disqualify me, but I wasn't good at faking anything. I'd learned in high school that I can't play poker – I'm too easily read.

For some reason it didn't occur to me to say I was gay. In my college years I'd been approached a number of times by gay men, seeing me as perhaps a member of the club. Being gay was still illegal then, so the approaches were gentle and tentative. I was flattered they were attracted to me, but I always politely declined. I wasn't interested, and my life was difficult enough already. Besides, I still held onto the idea that the military would help me figure things out.

Although I'm glad for much of the experience of going to Antioch – especially the co-op jobs – my first attempt at college was not a happy time for me. After the extra year, I finally managed to graduate – an event that was brought on more by wearing the school down than through any academic achievement of mine.

My parents had retired, sold their house, and moved into a 30-foot Airstream trailer. They roamed North America with no permanent address. I was jealous but I also felt even more untethered. They came by Ohio and took me to Denver to live with my sister and her family while I waited for the hammer to fall.

It didn't take long. It was 1967 and I was male, so only two weeks after getting to my sister's I got my draft notice. The Vietnam War was near its apex (or nadir). More and more men were being thrown into the effort in Southeast Asia to save the world from the spread of Communism, and the draft board saw me as a man.

I was still stuck on the idea of being an Air Force officer, perhaps a navigator. It seemed like a better deal than being a grunt in the jungles of Vietnam. I got a delay in reporting for the draft because they had wanted me to show up in Detroit, where I had registered for the draft, and I was living in Denver. The next draft notice said to report in Denver, but I got a delay for that while I was being evaluated by the Air Force. It turned out that I couldn't be an officer in the Air Force – one of my eyes was not correctable to 20/20. In fact, that eye meant I couldn't be an officer in any service except the Army. When I got my next draft notice, again wanting me to report in Detroit while still in Denver, I got another delay. By the time the fourth notice arrived, I knew my time was up and went to the Army recruiter. I thought I would be better able to guide my path if I enlisted rather than submitting to the draft, so I signed up.

Finally, I was sworn into the Army in Denver on November 1st, 1967. I was 24 years old. With the others who'd been sworn in that day, I flew to Fort Bliss in El Paso, Texas – my first time on an airplane. It was exciting. I'd thought about going into the military since my senior year of high school. The Army wasn't my first choice but it was what was available to me.

And it was scary – really scary. I was at their mercy. Would it be like the worst parts of gym class, where the others made fun of me for not being macho enough? Would I get lost in the faceless ranks? Would I be thrown into the maelstrom of Vietnam – coarsened, brutalized, killed?

I think most of our group on the plane were worried, not knowing what we were in for. One man started crying. Word came that he was a Polish national on some kind of visa that somehow made it possible for him to be swept up into our draft. It put things in perspective. Some of us may have been forced to put our lives on the line for our country, but at least it was *our* country.

(Let us not digress into the question of just what aspect of our country we were risking our lives for in the jungle 7,000 miles from home. That questioning wasn't helpful to those of us who were forced into that position.)

I found boot camp awful but manageable. The Army offered me a chance to be "one of the guys," probably for the first time in my life. My friends in boot camp called me Mr. Peabody, after one of the cartoon characters on television's "The Rocky and Bullwinkle Show." I didn't get the connection, so they explained it: Mr. Peabody, although a dog, wore glasses and was very smart. I was a little surprised I came across as smart, especially since I didn't get the reference right away, but I wore glasses and looked geeky enough to appear smart. And it was the first time I'd had a nickname since being Little Birdseed at the newspaper garage. It made me feel accepted – a rare feeling for me.

Despite some inadvertent self-sabotage, where I signed away my enlistment choice to apply for Officer Candidate School and only later decided I was better off not going to OCS, I was sent to Fort Knox to be trained as an armor crewman – a tanker. Six of us were offered a chance to go to Non-Commissioned Officers School for two weeks of leadership training before we started Armor School. Five of us agreed, seeing it as two more weeks before we would be sent to Vietnam, but the sixth man refused. He said he'd signed up to kill gooks and he wasn't going to waste any time. We all stepped back from him. Even the sergeant looked taken aback.

NCO School was like boot camp on steroids. We polished the sink drain pipes in the latrine. We made sure the hangers in our locker were all the same material and color, evenly spaced and facing the same way. We marched up and down. But the cooks' school was there, too, and the food was the best I had in the Army. (A low bar, certainly, but it was good.)

The five of us who'd gone through boot camp together and then leadership school were made squad leaders in the same company at Armor School. The school wasn't bad, especially for us squad leaders. I liked learning about the tanks, especially driving them. I tried not to think too hard about what they were for and the many ways they could be defeated.

Tanks had been developed during World War I for the trench warfare in Europe. They didn't do well in jungle terrain, so there were few of them in Vietnam. Most tanks were in Germany or Korea. Four of our group of five asked for Germany. The fifth decided to hedge his bets and asked for Korea, figuring he would get that for sure and the rest of us would go to Vietnam. They sent him to Korea and the other four of us to Germany. So much for trying to play the system.

I was trained as a tanker, but in then-typical Army style once I got to my duty station I was separated from the others and given a different job – one I wasn't trained for. They put me in charge of the company training program. I think it was probably because I was educated and had some office skills. I didn't particularly want to work in the motor pool anyway, but the promotion did set me apart. Again.

For a short period, one of my ancillary jobs was to be a jeep driver. Drivers are tasked with doing routine maintenance on their vehicles. After I ruined half the jeep's electrical system and melted most of one terminal off the 12-volt battery just trying to remove it from its compartment under the driver's seat, one of the mechanics told me that he'd maintain the vehicle for me if I promised to stay away from the jeep unless I was driving it. So it's probably just as well they had given me an office job.

The Army was (and is?) like a subset of the real world. It was much easier for me to see the machinery working and where the levers of power were. Less than a year after entering the Army, I was made an acting sergeant while still a private for pay. Perhaps they saw something in me I didn't see myself.

Trapped, some of us tried to think of ways to get out of it. One fellow I knew applied to Officer Candidate School. The school was 26 weeks long, and in order to pay the Army back for the time in training you had to extend your enlistment. I don't remember whether it was three or four years – four, probably. The commitment started when you entered the school. This fellow had heard that the top third of graduates went to active duty, the middle third to active reserve, and the bottom third to inactive reserve. His plan was to finish in the bottom third and thus be released from active duty. We heard later that he'd flunked out of the school two weeks before graduation and so was still an enlisted man but was committed to a longer term than before he had applied for school.

A man I knew from NCO and Armor schools was so bored with the duty in Germany, he volunteered as a door gunner in Vietnam. That seemed pretty drastic. Door gunners were not known for their longevity. I did hear indirectly that he made it home to Oregon, but I don't know if that was before or after his tour in Vietnam.

Being passive by nature and having been taught the worth and dignity of all people – a challenging belief at times – I thought of applying for conscientious objector status. But the more I looked into it, the less appealing it sounded. I would be moved to a non-combat job, which unofficially I already had, and open to the disdain, derision, and social bullying I feared. But the real problem was that my enlistment time – the countdown toward my release date – would be suspended while my application was being considered. It was conceivable that I would be held in limbo beyond my original release date while the bureaucracy ground slowly along. I decided I'd be better off just keeping my head down. And I was good at keeping my head down, or so I thought.

I loved Germany and disliked the Army. Protecting western Europe from the spread of Communism was, by and large, a mind-numbingly dull enterprise.

Any social system has official rules and unofficial rules. I could learn the official ones and at least pretend to be a straight arrow. The official rules gave me structure in a chaotic world. But I often had trouble picking up the unofficial rules and so could be socially awkward. The Army was no different, with its official and unofficial rules. But it was more of a closed system, where the unofficial rules were easier for me to discern.

And so the military suited me, oddly enough. Living as a man with a man's body and with a man's hormones when I should have a different body, different hormones, and a different position in society created a dissonance that made the world seem chaotic. I yearned for order, for alignment. The narrower, more structured life in the military satisfied some of that yearning. Even though I chafed at the restrictions, I asserted my individuality where I could and did well.

Our unit in Germany was divided into draftees and "lifers" – those who were making a career of the service. Each group held the other in disdain, and they had as little to do with each other as possible. Even though I had been promoted out of the motor pool, away from the others who were serving their first and only enlistment, I didn't join the ranks of the careerists.

The Army gave me plenty of opportunities to excel, but I wasn't able to take advantage of them. The draft-era Army of the 1960s was full of people who didn't fit in, who resented that they were there, resented the Army, resented the authority being imposed over them. Being an outsider myself and having my own issues, I gravitated toward these outsiders much to the detriment of any kind of career or benefit I might have gained from my Army time. Hungry for human contact, I fell in with bad company. There wasn't enough me in me yet to hold my own.

Living in an Army barracks in Germany, with inspections of all of my possessions now and then, I had no opportunity to cross-dress. For some reason, I didn't miss it. I was having enough trouble just coping with being in the Army. I explored clothing when not in uniform, but it was more countercultural than cross-gender.

The tedium of waiting for the Russians to invade Western Germany had dulled down many of us first-timers and allowed the careerists to play political games among themselves to pass the time. We had some excitement when Soviet tanks rolled into Prague in August, 1968. We didn't know if the tanks would keep rolling west to us and went on alert, ready to deploy to the field at a moment's notice. Somehow we learned that our main purpose was not to defeat the incursion but to slow it down long enough for reinforcements to be brought from the States. This lack of faith in our power wasn't encouraging. After a few weeks on alert, it became evident the tanks would stay in Czechoslovakia. We stood down, and our normal tedium returned.

The draftees who did well were those who knew who they were. That wasn't me. I wasn't self-directed enough to take advantage of my situation. When I was finally released from the Army, I knew I had not done well despite my advancement in rank. It was years before I would wear any piece of clothing that was any shade of green. Or examine too closely how I had failed myself.

5

IGNORING ✳ 1970-1983

"I never realized
till now
how hard the brain has to work
to make the body do what it asks.

Or maybe how hard the body has to work
to ignore
the brain."

— *Thalia Chaltas,* Because I Am Furniture

By the time I was released from the Army on Halloween, 1970, I felt completely unconnected to normal life. My parents continued to live in their 30-foot trailer with no fixed address; my brother was in North Carolina and my sister in Nebraska, both with young families; and I no longer knew anyone in my hometown of Detroit. My college roommate was in Boston, working a full schedule of teaching and research for his PhD while his wife was busy with their two year-old son and heavily pregnant with triplets. I went to Boston.

I stayed with Jim and his wife for a few days until I found a cheap furnished room nearby. Still not knowing what I wanted to do with my life, I got a job as Christmas help for a department store downtown. It paid nearly nothing, so I took several short-lived second jobs. Between my schedule and theirs, I saw little of Jim and his family. I was on my own. I had my hands full trying to establish my new life and didn't think about my questions around my gender. For me, it was like a Maslow Hierarchy, where my desire to be a woman fell below the day-to-day issues of finding housing and food, finding my way around a strange place, and dealing with a city full of people I didn't know.

Working at the department store, I met Valerie – a sweet girl of nineteen; I was 27. I had spent the last three years in exclusively male company, and I found Valerie's femininity very attractive. She was a fascinating mix of worldliness and innocence, was fun and smart, and I fell in love. Her father had made a career in the Army, and Valerie had lived in Japan and Italy, but she didn't know how to do a lot of things that I took for granted. Among other things, she couldn't drive a car, couldn't ride a bicycle, and had never written a check. But in some ways, she was a safe harbor in the chaos of navigating a strange city without connections.

My temporary job ended two days before Christmas, and I began looking for something more long-term. The week between Christmas and New Year's is not a good time to look for work, since most places are either shut down or working at half speed. With no money coming in and close to having to decide whether to sell my car or quit my apartment, I found a job as junior accountant at a small, family-owned chemicals distributor.

Even though we didn't work at the same store anymore, Valerie and I continued seeing each other. Our first date was to the Bunker Hill Monument because it cost only five cents to enter –

neither of us had much money. In the following months, we spent all of our free time together. We married Thanksgiving weekend, less than a year after we met. An instinct I didn't know I had kicked in – my gender issues stayed in the background as I took on this new role of husband.

Valerie had been raised Catholic and I had been raised Unitarian but neither of us attended church. We found a small Episcopal church we felt was a good compromise and were married by its priest, an agreeable man sensitive to our different backgrounds. The wedding was traditional, with Valerie in a white bridal gown and me in a three-piece blue suit I'd had made for me in Germany, but the ceremony was only loosely religious. Much of Valerie's large, extended family attended – including both of her grandmothers – along with my parents, my brother, and my sister and brother-in-law and their son. It was a moderate-sized wedding. We didn't have a lot of money to spend on it and didn't want something extravagant anyway.

During our courtship, I worked as the junior accountant at the chemical distribution company. Sometime after we were married, I transferred within the small company to dispatching their trucks – a good, manly job. I made the move because the dispatcher job paid better, but it was a job for which I was unsuited. (A word of advice: Don't take a job only because it pays better.) I could handle the logistics of it but didn't understand how long a delivery might take or how long it took to drive to the next one. And temperamentally I was completely unsuited for the Sisyphean nature of the work. Each day the trucks made pickups and deliveries. Each day they had to be scheduled for more pickups and deliveries. It was like "Groundhog Day," even though that movie wouldn't come out for another 20 years.

Unhappy, I found another junior accounting job and quit as dispatcher, but the new job fell through before I could start it. Unemployed, I flailed around, looking for work. My degree from

Antioch was in administration with a minor in accounting. I had liked the classes and with them I was finally able to graduate, but for some reason I held onto the idea that I wanted to work with my hands. I don't know why. I had done well at office work and was poor at other jobs. I'd tried to be a taxicab driver but lasted only one day. I tried pumping gas – self-service was several years in the future – and had managed to last two days before I quit. I applied for a job with a security company. They gently explained they needed someone who they could insert into a work situation – perhaps in a factory – who would fit in and be considered one of the group, kind of like a spy. And we both knew I couldn't do that. I tried to get into the skilled trades – electrician or perhaps brick-layer – but my college degree was a barrier, not to mention looking like someone who might get nicknamed Mr. Peabody.

My own family was scattered and not close. Married to Valerie, I was included easily into her large, very Italian, extended family, most of whom lived in the Boston area. Valerie and I saw them regularly. One afternoon we visited a cousin and her husband who had a new baby. It was like a switch got thrown within us. We had been happy without children, but being with this young family we were overcome with yearning for a baby of our own. Not thinking through our precarious circumstances, we decided to start a family.

Still without work, I saw an ad for the Coast Guard Reserve and went to see a recruiter. He encouraged me to consider active duty. After talking it over with Valerie, I decided to join the active-duty Coast Guard for technical training. Because of my Army training, he offered me gunner's mate – a good, manly job – but I didn't think I'd like the work. And I really couldn't see myself as a gunner's mate.

With my background in administration and accounting, he offered me storekeeper – supply clerks who managed inventory, purchasing, accounting, logistics, etc. I had learned enough from my Army experience to ask questions before I signed up for anything. The recruiter sent me to the local Coast Guard base to talk to the storekeepers.

I walked into their room and even though there were only five of them working away at their desks, all I could think of was a scene from Orson Welle's movie of Kafka's story "The Trial." It is one of those images that gets burned into your brain: It is black and white. The room is huge and without decoration – a warehouse or airplane hangar. At one end is a wooden platform one step up, with a single desk facing the room. The huge room is filled with desks, arranged rigidly in rank and file receding into the dim recesses in back. At each desk is a nondescript man in a plain business suit typing or writing or shuffling papers. A bell rings – like a school bell – and each man covers his typewriter, stands up, and leaves the room. I went back to the recruiter and asked what else he had.

He said my test scores were high enough I could be an electronics technician and sent me back to the base. This time I went into a warehouse. In the middle of the pallets and shelves was a lockable wire cage. The cage was filled with electronic gear – radios and who knows what else. There was a large workbench and three or four Coasties. One of them was in charge; the others were working there while they waited for their ships to come back to port or otherwise to keep them busy during some downtime. They had one of the radios tuned to a broadcast pop music station and talked and laughed and kidded each other as they worked. I went back to the recruiter and signed up for electronics school. Because I was married, Valerie had to sign some papers, too, saying she understood what we were getting into.

They sent me to a month-long boot camp in New Jersey, and then to electronics school on Governors Island, in New York Harbor. The school lasted almost five months, and during that time I moved Valerie down from Boston to a rented house on

Staten Island that we shared with two other couples. When I finished electronics school, I was offered a school where I would learn how to repair and maintain electronic cryptographic equipment. I could choose that or a track that would almost inevitably lead to isolated duty on some rock in the middle of one ocean or another. Valerie was pregnant by then, and I didn't want to risk having to abandon her by being sent on isolated duty. I chose crypto.

The training was at a Navy base in Vallejo, California. Valerie and I piled our belongings into our aging car, and I drove us across the country in four days during the November 1973 gas crisis. We found an apartment and I reported to school.

In California, our daughter Casey was born. I loved her from the moment she first appeared. We hadn't wanted to know her sex before she was born – such tests weren't common in those days. We just wanted a healthy baby, and Casey was just that. But I was relieved, too, that she was a girl. I didn't think I would know how to raise a boy – his spirit and needs would be beyond my understanding.

From crypto school, I was transferred to a ship home-ported back in New York City. I could live on the ship but we couldn't get Coast Guard housing on shore for Valerie and Casey for six months. We tried several different arrangements for them but none worked out. By the time we were able to get family housing on Governors Island, Valerie and I had moved six times in one year – twice while she was pregnant and four more in Casey's first year – sometimes living together and sometimes separately.

Like the Army, the Coast Guard was a structured system, but it offered me more autonomy and personal responsibility than the Army had. I'd learned a lot from my failures in the Army and did well. I loved the work – it was interesting and varied and challenging but within my capabilities. I loved the whole seafaring thing – the nautical names, the heritage, the whole idea of sailing the briny deep. I was respected and given a certain amount of latitude within the military structure. I loved the camaraderie. I loved the idea that we might be doing something worthwhile. I loved being part of a team. I loved that the Coast Guard was small and special – a military service not within the Department of Defense. I liked the fact that as long as I didn't screw up too badly, I would have a job – I might not know what it would be or where I'd have to go, but I didn't have to go job hunting. I liked that health care and educational opportunities were provided. It was a comfortable place for me and afforded me the opportunity to grow professionally and as a person.

My idea when joining the Coast Guard was to get the training and get out after my enlistment was up. But I liked the job and liked the life. Valerie and I talked about it. We agreed that I should re-enlist, but I ended up with five years of sea duty, first out of New York City, then out of Seattle.

Going to sea can be a humbling experience. Once out of sight of land, it is just the ship and the people on it. And the restless, living sea stretching horizon to horizon. One time in the middle of the North Atlantic I watched the waves as they looked like the famous Japanese print of curled waves with foam being blown off the tops. I lay on the steel deck of the ship trying to capture with my camera the feeling of that print, of what I saw, of what I felt. I realized that the sea was completely unconcerned with me, whether I was on it or under it, whether I existed at all. It gave me new perspective.

I loved being with Valerie and Casey. I loved seeing Casey grow. I was lucky enough to see her first steps. But I was gone a lot – almost two-thirds of the time. I seemed to compartmentalize it. I liked working on the ship. I liked being home with Valerie and Casey. But when I was away I didn't really miss them. When we were out, we were out until we came back. When I was in port, I was in port until the ship got underway.

I did feel guilt, though. Valerie ran the house but didn't have the background to do it. She had to take care of Casey and the finances and all the other things when the ship was out. She couldn't drive until we were in Seattle and a friend taught her. I taught her how to write a check but managing money was stressful for her. She really struggled at first, while I was having a good time sailing the Caribbean looking for drug smugglers or people who needed to be rescued. I would help her when I was in port, but I didn't take over from her. She developed a system that I didn't want to interfere with, that I didn't think it was right for me to try to interfere with.

At crypto school in Vallejo, California, and then once we got housing in New York and Seattle, Valerie and Casey were living among other Coast Guard families. Military service, whether active or as a dependent, is one of those kinds of life that is hard to understand unless you have lived it. Being with other Coast Guard families provided them a lot of support, especially the more subtle forms like emotional support and understanding what they were going through, that they wouldn't have gotten living with non-military people.

My gender issues remained in the background, waiting, while I juggled the roles of mariner, husband, and father. By the time I got shore duty, we had moved twice more and the marriage was pretty much over. With all the moves and my being away so much, I had failed my duty as protector. Plus, Valerie wanted a man for a husband, and I was finding it increasingly difficult to pretend to be one. I could play the role of a man and could usually pass as one, but I could never quite be one. I was male, but I never thought of myself as a man. I grasped the outlines of the role, but its subtleties eluded me. And the effort wore me down.

Valerie and I still got along well, and we worried about the effect of a divorce on Casey. But we knew that we would end up being miserable if we stayed together, and in the long run that would be worse for Casey. Wanting to make our separating as easy as possible, Valerie and I stayed together four more years as friendly companions. She enrolled in machinist training so she would be able to support herself. When the Coast Guard transferred me to a civilian shipyard in Tacoma, Washington, she was able to get a job as a machinist at the same shipyard. A woman machinist takes a lot of crap that I, disguised as a man, avoided.

We divorced while we were both working at the shipyard, when Casey was nine. In the eleven years we'd been married, we'd moved eleven times. When I was transferred to eastern Connecticut, Valerie had had enough and decided that she and Casey would stay on the West Coast. It was hard for me to leave Casey behind, but Valerie was a better parent than I was, having raised Casey while I was coming and going on the ships. Casey didn't understand the forces that were driving her parents apart and was hurt by our separation. I'm not sure Valerie and I understood it that well either; we just knew we needed to go our separate ways. It had been a terrible decision to have a baby when we did, but we loved Casey dearly. Years later, Casey told me that Valerie had explained to her that perhaps Valerie and I were meant to be together only long enough to have her. Indeed, Casey seems to have gotten the best parts of both of us, along with her own slant on things.

Thirty-five years later, I still remember the look on Casey's face when I left. It tore me apart, but I knew I had to leave. I couldn't stay as I was – I wasn't yet who I needed to be.

I sometimes wonder if the trajectory of my life was partly due to trying to be a regular man rather than this sometimes-confusing mix that I am. It could have been just trying to fit in, of course, and no more than that. But I've heard many stories of male-to-female transsexuals who worked to become muscular men and went for one of the more macho careers, to prove to the world and to themselves that they were, indeed, men. Unfortunately, when they could deny their real selves no longer, they were faced with transitioning in overdeveloped male bodies. I was fortunate that I did no more than play at bodybuilding and wear a beard when I could. In some ways, I was Mr. Peabody and used to my oddness.

6

EXPLORING ✳ 1983-1984

"Every dreamer knows that it is entirely possible to be homesick for a place you've never been to, perhaps more homesick than for familiar ground."
— Judith Thurman

After ten years in New York City and out west, I arrived in Connecticut on a glorious fall day. It was like a homecoming of sorts. I reported for work and found a house to rent in Rhode Island, 20 miles away. I needed a place with a garage – I had a motorcycle, a motorcycle with sidecar, and an old car I thought I could restore but never did. I had no drivable car.

Each of us goes through different phases in our lives. Some are subtle shifts that we might not recognize until afterwards. Some are obvious. This one was obvious. I had been married, living with my family; now I was single, living alone. I had been a technician, working with what was. Now I was at the Research and Development Center, working with what might be. I had been enlisted, working my way up from Seaman to Chief Petty Officer – an NCO.

Now I was a Warrant Officer – a whole different animal within the military structure.

And I had turned forty. I became very aware – suddenly, it seemed – that my life might be half over, and if I was going to do something with it I'd better get started. A satellite campus of Rensselaer Polytechnic Institute offered evening classes next to the R&D Center. Aware of my limited remaining lifespan, and with my evenings free and stationed ashore, I signed up for graduate school.

I loved my new job and spent several evenings during the week taking classes. On weekends I was happy exploring the area on my motorcycle. But that still left me with time on my hands. I lived alone some distance from work and had no social life other than while at work or school. Left to my own devices in the privacy of my home, I began to dress in women's clothes to comfort myself. Over the next few months, I crossdressed as often and as much as I could. I bought most things at stores – the larger the store the better, giving me some sense of anonymity. I also bought some things from catalogs. On-line shopping didn't exist back then. But I had to be careful, because I couldn't try things on and it was hard enough to buy them the first time. Going back and explaining why the item wasn't right would be too hard. I remember just once carrying a skirt across the store to the men's dressing rooms to try it on.

I didn't want to spend a lot of money for clothes I would wear only in private. I didn't try thrift stores very often. I find the relative chaos of them difficult to deal with, and the clerks are not as professional – they were more likely to give me the hairy eyeball. It took years before I was relatively comfortable shopping for women's clothes as a man. Sometimes I'd make up a little story about my wife, but the younger clerks weren't interested and the older ones probably saw through my subterfuge.

I bought underwear and stockings and blouses and skirts and, once in a while, a dress or jacket. I gradually acquired a pretty good wardrobe. It was more about how I felt and how I thought I looked – how I could convince myself how I looked – than how I actually looked.

I didn't understand why I had this need or why wearing women's clothes was such a comfort. Trying to understand, I looked for information. It was, of course, before the internet, a time when you had to go to the information rather than being able to bring it to you. I was living in Westerly, Rhode Island – a small town with a wonderful library. Surprisingly, I found a trove of information about gender and transsexuality there. I found auto-biographies of transsexuals – the travel writer Jan Morris, the Chicago journalist Nancy Hunt, and the tennis player Renée Richards[1]. There were also older papers by the pioneering endocrinologist Dr. Harry Benjamin, and more recent scientific papers. I read everything the library had and began to think about transitioning and living as a woman.

But I had no idea how to go about doing it. I had no idea how to find a doctor. I didn't know what I would need. There were no support groups that I was aware of. I didn't know how to find anyone to help me through the process. I had no money and no way to pay for any of it. And for some reason I didn't even consider the problem of my facial hair. Transitioning would mean leaving everything I knew. Certainly I would have to leave the Coast Guard, and I loved being in the Coast Guard.

I was very afraid that I would always be identifiable as having been male. I could believe I looked like a woman when I was crossdressing, but that was part of the fantasy. I didn't think I would be so believable to others. As far as I knew, I'd never seen a transsexual in person, and I'd seen very few pictures. I'd seen a picture of Christine Jorgensen in a showgirl outfit and I'd seen drag queens, but I wondered about ordinary women. Morris' book had a before and an after picture, and Richards' book had a few, but there were no pictures in Hunt's book.

In so-called adult bookstores, I'd seen magazines with pictures of people who evidently had been born male but had long hair and breasts. These would be posed naked, showing their penises and testicles, which were made smaller by the female hormones but were still very much there. The models tried to look appealing, enticing, seductive. The images are burned into my brain forever, but I've managed to erase the label used for these souls. I didn't want to be one of them. Besides, I was already forty years old. No amount of surgery or hormones would give me a young, wispy body like theirs.

For me, it wasn't about my body. I was used to my male body, pretty much. I wanted to live in the world as a woman and to be seen by the world as a woman. If I could never achieve that, it wasn't worth it to me to make the attempt. I was already odd enough without becoming a caricature or an obvious imitation of a woman. And as someone identifiably male but wearing women's clothes and claiming to be a woman, I was afraid I would be unemployable and a social outcast. I thought it very likely that I would have to live in poverty, on the fringes of society where life can be brutal. I knew I couldn't turn to show business as Christine Jorgensen had – that was way beyond my capabilities. From the magazine pictures and somehow in other ways, I knew that some men are attracted to women who are really boys. I was afraid I might have to turn to prostitution – a really dangerous way to live. I was torn between my longing and my fear.

(A 2017 New York Times article[2] stated that 80% of transgender people in Brazil rely on prostitution to survive. They didn't write about such things in 1984, but that doesn't mean it wasn't happening.)

I wrote Valerie about my dilemma. She wrote back sympathetically, but she worried about our daughter. Casey had just lost her father geographically, and losing him to become a woman would make the separation all the more difficult. And Valerie knew that my transition would end my Coast Guard career. She didn't want me to make a rash decision that would lose the years I'd invested. She asked me to wait until Casey was older.

I agreed. It was an easy out for me. Now I had a reason not to step off that cliff.

Having decided that I couldn't transition, I stuffed myself back into the closet. I did decide, however, to stop confining myself to what I thought of as straight male behavior. I was going to try to relax a little. If I appeared to be gay, then so what? This purposeful small loosening of the laces helped me pull myself back from the brink.

The idea of transitioning was unrealistic – a fairy tale. I convinced myself I was a crossdresser. Just a crossdresser. I could be satisfied with just the clothes, or so I thought. I didn't think I was a different person when I was dressed in a skirt and heels – I was still just me – but the dressing up calmed me, at least for a while. Then I'd need to dress up again. I hoped it wasn't a fetish, because being a fetish, I thought, would mean there was something wrong with me. And I didn't think there was anything wrong with me. I was just screwed up, that's all.

7

DELUDING ✳ 1984-2001

"You can fool yourself, you know. You'd think it's impossible, but it turns out it's the easiest thing of all."
— Jodi Picoult, *Vanishing Acts*

In the early spring of 1984, after I'd been in Rhode Island for about six months, my parents drove up from their home in North Carolina for a several-day visit. They wanted to see where I lived and, probably, to check how I was doing as being newly-divorced. In my rented house I had room for them to stay with me.

During their visit, my father had a heart attack. He was 78 years old; my mother was 76. My father was in the hospital for several days. My mother spent as much time as she could with him. It is the only time I ever saw my mother close to breaking.

My father came home to my place when they released him from the hospital. He was advised not to travel. Being familiar with the story "The Man Who Came for Dinner" just as I was, they were very good at not encroaching on me. I was working full time and taking grad school classes at night. I came and went pretty freely. Sometimes my mother would cook for me. Sometimes I would wear my women's clothes under my long bathrobe.

My mother stayed with my father most of the time. She may have gone grocery shopping, or maybe she relied on me – I don't remember. But she stayed close to home. One weekend she said, "We can't go to church, so why don't you go and tell us what it was like." I went, taking my sidecar rig since my bike was in the shop.

At the Unitarian Universalist church in East Greenwich, Rhode Island, one of the people I met was Polly. She was vice president of the congregation and invited me to a newcomer gathering at the parsonage that Wednesday evening. Wanting to get to know people in the church, I went to that, too, but spent most of the evening talking only to her. The next Sunday I had my bike back and rode it to church, carrying an extra helmet. I asked Polly if she wanted to go for a ride after church. She agreed, and we spent a couple of hours riding around the back roads of Rhode Island.

My parents stayed with me for what turned out to be two months, after which I drove them back to North Carolina in their car. Since I had no workable car of my own and had been commuting to work by motorcycle through the winter, they took pity on me and sold me their second car, which I drove back to Rhode Island.

Back in Rhode Island, Polly and I began seeing more and more of each other. I was still crossdressing when alone. Polly lived near Providence and I was in the southwest corner of the state. It was only 43 miles between us, but in Rhode Island that's a long way. We usually saw each other only on weekends.

We were edging toward marriage, but I was wary after being divorced so recently. Not ready to commit to a ring, for Christmas I gave her diamond studs for her ears. Very small diamonds, but diamonds nonetheless.

One Sunday afternoon sometime after Christmas, together at my place I was feeling squishy – how I would get when I was uncertain of myself, when I was having trouble managing, trouble navigating life. I don't know what had preceded it and why I was feeling that way. Polly was standing at the sink in the kitchen. I came out of the bedroom in a full, mid-length Kelly green skirt. She looked at me and said: "I like you better in pants." That pretty much was that.

I told her about my dressing. I didn't tell her about thinking about transitioning. That was no longer relevant, since I wasn't going to do it and now I was just a crossdresser. She accepted it, I think. At least I thought so until years later. Some weeks later, perhaps still digesting this fact of me, as we were driving somewhere she turned to me and said, "You *are* heterosexual, aren't you?" I said I was, and that seemed to satisfy her.

We married in late May of that year. It was a small affair in our backyard. Most of Polly's extended family lived in Rhode Island, but she didn't want any of them at the wedding. So to be fair I didn't invite any of my family except for Casey. She had recently turned eleven and flew across the country to be with us for the ceremony.

Everyone wore party clothes and the reception was a potluck. The minister of our church officiated. Polly had a close friend as her matron of honor. Polly and I had become close to a couple of men from the church who had gotten together about the same time we had. One of them served as my best man; the other loaned me his sport jacket. There were no other attendants.

These two men – Dan and Steve – have continued to be good friends. I was always relaxed with them. At the time, I didn't tell them about my crossdressing or my now-suppressed desire to transition. But through our friendship they opened a door to a different kind of world for me, and I began to wonder if I might be gay. It seemed entirely possible. But the problem with that idea was that I was never interested in being with a man. I had had those offers when I was younger but just wasn't interested. Now in my forties, I was finding it harder to play the role of a straight man, so I thought about being a gay man. I thought I wouldn't have to hold myself in so tightly, could show emotion, could be a little outrageous, could be a little looser. But I was attracted only to women, which was probably disqualifying and made the whole idea confusing.

When we were first married, Polly and I had fun with my crossdressing. Sometimes we would go window-shopping for women's clothes together. One of us would point at something and say, "That would look better on you." The other of us would spot something else and respond, "And that would look better on you." Sometimes she would ask me to explain my need to crossdress, but I couldn't explain something I didn't understand myself.

She came to resent having to keep this family secret a secret. Her father was an alcoholic, and growing up she had felt the burden of keeping that secret. She didn't like assuming yet another secret that wasn't even about her. I wasn't brave enough to go out in public dressed – I didn't think I could carry it off. And I had a position of some responsibility in the Coast Guard. Discovery could jeopardize how we lived. She just wanted to pretend I wasn't this way, even though I was.

My billet at the R&D Center was for four years, but I got a six-month extension to finish school. We'd had to move to another rented house because our landlady wanted to move back to town, but I was in Westerly for four and a half years – the longest I'd been anywhere since leaving my parents' house to go to college, 27 years earlier.

With my brand new master's degree, I had thought I had arranged a transfer to a Coast Guard computer lab in Virginia, but it was not to be. I got a call from the detailer – the man responsible for balancing our individual desires with the needs of the service. He offered me four choices – all overseas and all of them outside of my area of expertise. (Polly and I had spent the evening before at a concert by a bassoon quartet. For years I wondered if there was some astral connection between the four bassoons playing alone together and the four choices, but I finally gave up the conjecture as fruitless.) I told the detailer that I'd had five years sea duty and had done my time away. He pointed out that I'd been ashore stateside for nine years and it was my turn for less desirable duty.

Polly had had no experience with military life. With me working at what was essentially a civilian job at the R&D Center and with us living in town, she wasn't exposed to it. I shopped for groceries at the Navy base near my work, but she rarely went with me. When we'd married I'd tried to explain that the Coast Guard could send me anywhere – a ship or an isolated island in the middle of nowhere. "Oh no," she'd say. "You're too valuable for them to do that." She didn't get it.

Three of the four choices the detailer offered me were unaccompanied tours. Iwo Jima and Hokkaido were unaccompanied because the Coast Guard had no facilities to handle families and there was no base nearby. The island of Attu, on the west end of the Aleutian Chain, was truly isolated, with the only inhabitants the dozen or so Coasties staffing the radio-navigation station there.

The fourth choice was Iceland. It was an accompanied tour because it was on the NATO base operated by the US Navy and had housing, a hospital, a school, even a small movie theater. Both Polly and I knew that if I went off to an isolated station for a year, she wouldn't be there when I got back. I chose Iceland.

Being a single parent has to be one of the most difficult things anyone does. Casey was a good kid – smart, healthy, well-behaved – but she also had just turned fourteen. Valerie, who'd had Casey for ten months of each of the last five years, had had enough. Casey was going to Iceland too.

So off we went: Polly, who had a hippie's view of the military and who resented being labeled a dependent, having to know my Social Security number for her to cash a check, and resentful of having been thrown into the role of parent; Casey, struggling as most teenagers do, uprooted from her friends and school to live in a remote land with a stepmother who was awkward in that role; and me, put into a job I didn't want and felt completely unqualified for, trying to manage a household of two women who at times struggled to get along. Part of my job involved weeklong trips to stations in Greenland or a tiny island in the Norwegian sea or somewhere else far away. I'd leave Casey and Polly to work it out between themselves. It was an interesting time.

Polly got a job as director of the adult education program on base, which gave her some status in her own right. And Casey got into the Model UN program at school and was the youngest to succeed in doing all the work needed to qualify for a group trip to a conference in Brussels. I muddled through my job and role as father.

Casey went home to her mother after the first year. Things were a little less complicated then. I had settled into my job but still didn't know what I was doing. Unknown to me, Polly had gotten on tranquilizers or antidepressants, although she still had episodes of instability. I loved Iceland and the Icelanders I worked with, but those two years were a hard passage.

In Iceland I had no opportunity to crossdress and, in fact, never even thought of it. There was too much going on, and my gender issues were submerged while I tried to handle more immediate problems.

By 1991, Polly and I were back in the States, living outside of Frederick, Maryland. Our friends from Rhode Island, Dan & Steve, would visit every year after Christmas on their way to spend their winter in Florida. One evening when they were with us, I put on a skirt and came into the living room. Other than Valerie and Polly, they were the first I came out to. I don't know that it changed things much other than that after that both Polly and I were able to talk with them about my crossdressing.

In 1993, they came to stay with us so they could go to the March on Washington for Lesbian, Gay and Bi Equal Rights and Liberation. (In 1993 it was just LGB.) I was pretty sure I wasn't gay, since I had no interest in being with a man, but I wasn't so sure I was straight, either. Regardless, I wanted to go with them and participate in the march.

Dan and Steve and I rode the Metro into Washington, to All Souls Unitarian Church for a rousing service with Unitarian Universalists from all over, including most of the national leadership. We then changed into rally clothes with a crowd of others in the men's room and trooped down to the National Mall. It was an exciting, exhilarating, exhausting day. We left before it all ended, worn out but still high from the excitement. Riding the escalator down to the trains, I told the guys that I didn't think I was gay – I just liked to wear women's clothes. The young woman ahead of us turned around and happily said her group just used the word "queer."

Yes: queer. The word had long been used as a pejorative, but when unloaded it became an umbrella term that included all of us who are not hetero- and gender-normative. I liked it. It made me part of a large group of interesting and intriguing people. It gave me an identity and pulled me in from the lonely periphery.

Still, I just thought I was odd. I wasn't ready to be out as queer, even to myself. I didn't recognize it at the time, but saying in public that I liked to wear women's clothes within hearing of the stranger ahead of us was another small crack in my carapace.

As the years passed, it became more difficult for me to suppress my needs. What I came to call my gender dysphoria – the misalignment of who I was with the life role I felt compelled to play – became ever stronger. I thought of it as being always "out of register," where the colors of an image don't line up. The constant background fog of my dysphoria made navigating life a challenge. Somehow, dressing in women's clothes offered me a break from that feeling. Because I couldn't wear the clothes outside the house, it didn't make life more comprehensible – didn't align the colors or clear the fog – but it gave me respite, a small time when I didn't have to deal with it, didn't have to pretend I was a man.

By this time, I was buying most of my women's clothes from catalogs. Because I was dressing only for my own pleasure and never went anywhere in the clothes, I bought inexpensive things. And of course because I was shopping mail-order, I got more and more catalogs. (We got so many that at one point the mailman asked us to get a larger box out on the road.) I went through the catalogs, looking for things that might be appropriate. In one of them I found what were billed as "breast enhancers" – bra inserts made of foam rubber molded to look like breasts. The back of the insert was concave, to fit over one's own breast. I could get a set for less than $40.

When I wore a bra during my dress-up times, I would just stuff something in it to give me a bit of a shape. I had found that using nylon underwear as stuffing was the most comfortable and, being squishy, worked the best. When I got the foam rubber "enhancers" I inserted them and, well, it's hard to describe. They felt so good, so right. I didn't understand why that should be so, but it was deeply satisfying, more so than what I got just from dressing. Perhaps I should have clued in that there was more going on than just finding a cheap set of falsies, but I didn't.

When I retired from the Coast Guard in 1994, I was going to be a house husband, staying home and taking care of the house. We were living in exurbia and no one was around during the day. I used the time alone to wear a house dress, but that meant I had to stay inside, alone. It was terribly isolating – I lasted a month before looking for paid work.

I found a job on the nearby Army base, doing computer work

for a contractor to the Department of Defense (DoD). The job was less than ten minutes away – close enough that I could go home for lunch – but it wasn't a good fit for me. I could do the technical requirements of the work but they were outside my area of interest and I found the secure facility oppressive. Worst of all was a co-worker who was suspicious of me from my first day, who resented my work in what he considered his area. With some success, he worked on making my life increasingly miserable.

As the atmosphere at work became more intolerable, I began dressing during my lunches at home. I didn't have much time, but dressing up would comfort me and settle me. It got to be a regular thing – rush home, dress, prepare and eat lunch, change back to work clothes, and rush back. The dressing midday calmed me and made going back to work easier. But as the work situation worsened and I needed the midday dressing just to get through the day, I began looking for another job.

I applied for a programming job with a Coast Guard contractor in West Virginia, a half hour from my home. I made it clear that the kind of work I was doing for DoD was outside my area of strength and I would not do it. They assured me I would be working only as a programmer and systems analyst. I agreed and they hired me. At my going-away party at the DoD job, the management announced publicly that I would always be welcome to come back – a rather remarkable statement. Usually it's pretty easy for people to read me, but they must have missed the signs. I wasn't just moving on; I was fleeing.

With the new job I couldn't go home and dress at lunchtimes anymore, but I had a job I enjoyed and didn't have the need to relieve workplace stress every few hours. However, I did start dressing a bit before work. I would put on a skirt and sit on the garden bench with my morning coffee before Polly and, hopefully, the neighbors were awake. Autumn was the best, because it was still warm but stayed dark late enough that I felt safe.

The pressure inside me to dress in women's clothes kept increasing. I took advantage of whatever opportunities I had to dress, but I know that the more frequent dressing was a result, not the cause, of the pressure.

For some reason, I always resisted the idea I was a woman in a man's body, that I was in the wrong body. I also resisted the idea that I needed to "express my feminine side" – a common cross-dressing refrain. I just felt the need to dress whenever I had an opportunity. It was, perhaps, the inner me pushing to break free. At this point in my life, that inner clamoring expressed itself as the desire to wear women's clothes – skirts, stockings, heels, soft blouses, nylon underwear, jewelry. It was those items that were forbidden to me as a male in our culture. I had tried wearing women's pants when I was younger, hoping no one would notice, but I didn't find them satisfying.

Sometime after starting work for the Coast Guard in West Virginia, I stumbled on a magazine put out by Renaissance, a mid-Atlantic association of male crossdressers. They had a few chapters west of the Appalachians but most were around their center, near Philadelphia. The magazine had pictures of crossdressers – G-rated pictures, always fully clothed, not trying to look sexy. But I was more interested in the articles and stories. It also had ads for specialty shops and I bought some decidedly uncomfortable things like a girdle with padded hips. But mostly I bought my clothes from mainstream department stores and catalogs.

Renaissance didn't have an internet forum – personal computers weren't common yet – but they did have a pen pal system. I joined in. I was living in Maryland, working in West Virginia. Not wanting to be identifiable and perhaps being a bit paranoid, I got a post office box near my work. Now I had to come up with a name. I'd never had a woman's name for myself. I didn't think of my dressed up self as separate from my male self. I was just me – a better, more comfortable me, but still me.

If my parents had recognized me as a girl, I would have been named Elizabeth, after my mother's favorite sister. I thought I could use some variation of that for my name. I settled on Betty, thinking of Betty Boop and Betty Friedan and maybe Betty Ford. It wasn't a good choice, but it was just an alias; I didn't think of myself as being Betty.

The Renaissance chapter nearest to me was in the Virginia suburbs of DC. After my times with Albert in his basement back in Detroit, I had always dressed in isolation. I considered going to a meeting of the Virginia group. I wrote and explained that I sported a full beard. Someone wrote back that I wouldn't be welcome because some of their members were still struggling with how they were hurt by the cultural norms and me showing up in women's clothes and a beard could be more than they would be able to manage.

I read in the Renaissance magazine that they were going to have a dinner for members at a hotel in eastern Pennsylvania. Considering it an opportunity to dress, I wrote to be sure my hairy face would be OK. They were more welcoming than the Virginia group had been and wrote that all were welcome, regardless of where they were on their own journey. I still wondered whether I should go. Polly encouraged me – I could dress however I liked and would be three hours away from her. I was hesitant, but it seemed worth a try.

I reserved a room at the hotel where the dinner would be held. Once there, I dressed carefully in my room. With the beard, I didn't use any makeup. Anxious, I walked through the halls on my way to the event room. I saw only one person, and he showed no reaction as I walked past him in my beard, skirt and heels. I must have been quite a sight, but he at least pretended to be unfazed. At the event room, I was welcomed, handed a drink, and left to mingle. It was my first time dressing in public and the first time I'd ever been with men I knew were crossdressers. There were some wives and other supporters, but the group was mostly male cross-dressers in full femme.

After dinner, the smaller group I was with decided to go down to the hotel bar. I went with them down the elevator and through the lobby but stopped at the door to the bar. The place was full of what looked a bit like a large frat party. Very aware of my beard, I backed into the hall and went to my room. I heard later that the bar had fallen silent when the group of crossdressers walked in. Then it had burst into applause.

While I was working for the Coast Guard contractor in the late 90s, I spent a day at the Johns Hopkins Sex and Gender Clinic. For years I'd heard of this clinic, one of the few in the country. I thought that since I was living in Maryland I should take advantage of the proximity.

I made an appointment for an evaluation and drove the hour-plus to the hospital. I filled out lots of forms and answered lots of written questions. I wanted them to tell me what was going on with me, why I had these feelings of being off-kilter most of my life, but they didn't seem to know what to do with me. I was outside their notion of who needed their help – I was successful in my marriage and my career, I wasn't addicted to drugs or alcohol, I had no police record, and I wasn't suicidal. I was just a normal person, evidently male, who liked to dress in women's clothes. Why was I even there? After being there for several hours, I asked myself that, too. The only benefit I got from the day-long experience was when a counselor said in exasperation, "But lots of men wear women's clothes!"

They asked if I would be willing to talk to a group of interns. Wanting to help them learn a little if I could, I agreed. I was left alone in a room with nothing to do for an hour or so, presumably while the group gathered. I don't do well just waiting, especially if I have nothing – and I mean nothing – to do. Smartphones were still more than five years away, and with nothing to read or write or look at, I withdrew into myself. When I was finally called to the room where the group had gathered, I sat facing a semi-circle of more than a dozen people in white lab coats. They asked questions and I answered, probably with little animation after being dulled down by the waiting. The clinic director badgered me some, perhaps to break through my withdrawal and perhaps to crack me to reveal the psychosis I was hiding, but I held my ground, refusing to be baited. Finally, he advised me to stay away from crossdressers, as if that would solve my problems. I didn't think much of him.

By the time I left the clinic I was in a daze. I found my car and pulled up to the exit kiosk to pay. The woman in the kiosk had the longest fingernails I'd ever seen, extending at least an inch beyond the ends of her fingers. How she managed to get them that long and how she managed to live with nails that long, I have no idea. She carefully placed my change in my palm using the edges of her fingers. It was a surreal end to a dreadful day.

Leaving the hospital at last, I plunged into the Baltimore rush hour traffic. By the time I got home I had tucked much of the experience away in my vault labeled "Experiences Not to Examine Too Closely." I had gone for help and found confusion, mind-numbing boredom, exposure, and verbal abuse. So much for the famed Johns Hopkins Sex and Gender Clinic.

The Renaissance magazine included letters from members – a precursor to the internet forums of today. Someone had written in about how he had figured out how to put on earrings that appeared to be for pierced ears using a dab of Super Glue. I thought that was a little silly – why didn't he just get his ears pierced? I don't know why I thought having pierced ears would be no big deal. I had spent much of my life trying to fit in and do what I thought was expected of me. At the time, few men had pierced ears – just a few outliers like pirates and gay men and perhaps a few rockers. But there had been enough of a cultural shift for it to be (barely) acceptable for men to have pierced ears. The convention was to have only one pierced. Supposedly, a pierced left ear indicated you were gay, and a pierced right one meant you were straight. But I think that was only in the Northeast, and in the South it was the other way around. Or maybe it was the right ear in the Northeast and left ear in the South that was the gay signal. I was never able to remember which was which, and I'm not sure most other people knew either. But I wasn't trying to signal anything. I really didn't care whether people saw me as gay or straight. Regardless of the gay-straight signals, I wanted both ears pierced for the simple reason that I wanted to wear earrings when I wore women's clothes.

Pierced ears were Polly's gift to me for my 54th birthday. I still have the gold-colored studs they used to do it. When I showed up at work with both ears pierced, my counter-culturally savvy boss said I had both of them pierced because I couldn't decide which one to have done, implying I couldn't decide whether to be straight or gay. I accepted her explanation and used it later from time to time.

Polly had been dirt poor during parts of her life and had learned how to save money. She taught me how to save, too. After I retired from active duty in the Coast Guard, both Polly and I had good-paying jobs and managed to save enough that we could retire in '01, as soon as she was eligible. I had the best job I'd ever had, but we wanted to tour on our motorcycle. As it turned out, while we were trying to decide whether to retire at our first opportunity or work longer and salt more money away, we got into conversations with several strangers. They each said: "Do it now. You never know what will happen."

So in the spring of '01, I quit my job and Polly retired. We hopped on our motorcycle and set off across the country. We had no agenda other than to ride until we didn't want to anymore. We had our house in Maryland and a house in Rhode Island that we were renting out until we moved there, but when we got to the Rocky Mountains we started thinking of moving west. When we stopped for a visit at my sister's house near Denver, I searched the internet for towns in the West that had both a university or college and a Unitarian Universalist fellowship or church. We may not attend classes, and we'd been to enough different UU churches to know that they are not all the same, but I thought that a town with both a college and a UU church would say something about the town, even if we didn't go to either one. We began riding to all the towns on my list.

By the time we got home to Maryland again, three months later, we had decided to move to Laramie, Wyoming instead of Rhode Island. For some reason, on the road, on the bike, my gender issues were quiet, waiting to resurface once I settled down again. I had been wearing underwear without a fly for several years by then, which meant I had to sit or, outdoors, squat to pee; but otherwise I didn't think about it at all.

8

SURVIVING ✳ 2001-2007

"Sometimes even to live is an act of courage."
— Lucius Annaeus Seneca

We moved to Laramie in early December, 2001. It was cold but clear and sunny – weather I would learn was common in the winter. (When I had called the telephone company from Maryland to set up phone service at our new home, the agent, evidently based in Southern California, had laughed. "You're moving to Laramie in *December*?") There was a little light snow the day our furniture arrived but the winds were relatively mild. Polly and I started the now-familiar cycle of moving – the excitement of setting up a new home, exploring the neighborhood and area, meeting new people.

We had moved knowing no one in town. We introduced ourselves to our next door neighbors. They were delighted to see us. Our house had been a rental for some years, with a changing assortment of young college men prone to loud parties and poor upkeep. They thought we would be better neighbors.

Polly and I spent December setting up the house and exploring. We waited until after Christmas to go to the UU fellowship. When we did go, we sat next to the door, to facilitate a quick escape if needed. But we were warmly welcomed and quickly felt integrated into the church.

Laramie is a small town. It is the smallest town I've lived in other than when I went to Antioch, but there I'd been at school and wasn't part of the town. And Laramie sits by itself on a high plain between mountains. The nearest town is 50 miles away, with a lot of open land in between. I once heard a man describe it to his son as "Laramie is a size where when you go into town you always see someone you know but you don't know everyone you see."

Polly and I were happy together, happy to be in Laramie, happy to be able to ride the motorcycle as much as we wanted. But we were both retired now, and a bit at loose ends. Left to our own devices, I began dressing more often. And Polly, without my noticing, began drinking more.

My crossdressing seemed to be a second-tier activity. In the Army and on the Coast Guard ships, all of my belongings were open to inspection. I didn't have any women's clothes with me and didn't miss them. On the ship I was one of the two electronics technicians (ETs) who kept the radios going. My rank was on my collar or my sleeve. I fit into the community and the hierarchy. As an ET, I wasn't expected to be particularly manly or macho. I was expected to be smart and capable.

And on the motorcycle, with severely limited space to carry things, I never took any women's clothes. But as they were on the ship, my gender issues remained quiet. Maybe it was because the riding engaged me so thoroughly. Maybe because as a motorcyclist I knew who I was, with my helmet and riding suit and boots – like when I wore my Coast Guard uniform. These uniforms proclaimed who I was. Not the totality of who I was, but they gave me an anchor to which to cling. Besides, I needed a private space to dress, and private time.

But neither condition was sustainable. The ship would come back to port; the motorcycle trip would end. And real life would resume. When I was away too long – either on the ship or the bike – I would begin to miss my shoreside or home connections. That really became evident when we moved to Laramie and could set our own schedule. A big part of retirement was to have the time to ride, but after riding a while I would miss the Laramie connections – the friends, the house, the church, the town. Then after a while at home I would miss the riding, the traveling, the road, the serendipity of meeting strangers. The challenge was to balance the two. If we were gone too long, the town connections became more tenuous than I liked. If I stayed at home too long, I missed being on the road. I needed the grounding of home, but I also needed the time away.

And when I was back home, dressed as an ordinary man, pretending to be one, I had a more difficult time knowing who I was. And when I had a more difficult time, I would fall back to crossdressing.

I dressed up inside the house when Polly was out. Sometimes I wore a few things under my regular clothes but somehow that wasn't satisfying. We lived in town. I fantasized about having a place out in the wide-open spaces, away from everything, where I could dress freely. Besides the fact that Polly wouldn't have gone along with it, I knew that being that alone wouldn't be good for me. Even dressing inside the house meant I couldn't answer the door, and I found that isolating. It would be a very poor solution to what was going on in me.

Polly had always loved her red wine and had always drunk more than I did. I hadn't thought much about it, but it became evident there were problems as we settled into retirement. When we had been working she only drank in the evening, or so I thought. But now she wanted two glasses of wine with her lunch and would be upset if I wanted to have lunch somewhere that didn't serve wine. She had always had bridge anxiety and began carrying wine in a water bottle to sip before we were to cross a long or high bridge. Or she'd drink a little in the middle of the night if she couldn't sleep.

Submerged in my own issues, I didn't pay much attention to it. It was annoying at times, but she was an adult and responsible for her own behavior. Looking back on it now, I wonder at my cluelessness. But there have been times in my life when I wore my cluelessness like armor, protecting me from realities I wasn't equipped to handle.

Gradually Polly's drinking increased and problems with her drinking became more evident. I was still too naive to be alarmed – or too self-absorbed. Maybe both. I had no experience with someone who had a drinking problem and didn't recognize the signs.

One day riding our bicycles back from lunch downtown, Polly lost her balance and crashed to the ground. I pulled her bike out of the traffic lane and helped her up. But I wasn't sympathetic. Struggling with my own issues, I wasn't yet strong enough to support her with hers. I gave the appearance of strength, but a lot of that was just my will to hold myself together.

In November, Polly collapsed when leaving the restaurant after lunch. She'd had her usual two glasses of wine. We'd walked downtown, so I hurried home to get the car. I called the doctor. I explained what had happened and my concern. Something was wrong. For her, two glasses of wine should barely take the edge off.

Before then I don't know that I'd ever seen Polly drunk. To me – naive me – you were either drunk or not drunk, and drunks acted silly or mean or fell asleep. I was just beginning to realize it wasn't that cut and dried.

Things went downhill from there. In the following April, Polly and I got into a big argument and she stormed out of the house. Evidently she went to our friend Sarah's, because after midnight Sarah let herself into our house, woke me up, and told me Polly had checked herself into the psych ward at the hospital. By the next afternoon, Polly called me to pick her up. Since she'd checked herself in, she could check herself out. Now even I had woken up to the fact of her problem.

They'd done some blood work on Polly while she was in the hospital. A week later we learned it wasn't just alcohol attacking her liver – she had hepatitis C, too. We sought more specialized help.

The liver specialist we found in Colorado prescribed chemotherapy, but he wouldn't start the treatments until Polly had been dry for 60 days. He said it wouldn't be worth the effort if she was just going to keep destroying her liver with alcohol. After a number of false starts, Polly managed 60 consecutive dry days with only a two-day relapse in the middle that she wouldn't mention to the doctor. She started chemo.

Polly was miserable. The chemo made her sick, and not being able to drink made it many times worse. I didn't know how to help other than to feed her and listen to her complaints and make sure she was as comfortable as possible. But I couldn't stand to stay with her all the time and tried to carve out some time for myself. By the end of the third week she decided the chemo wasn't worth it. She said there was only a fifty-fifty chance it would help anyway. And life without wine wasn't worth it either. She stopped the chemo and resumed drinking with a vengeance.

I could do nothing. She would never accept advice from me, would reject out-of-hand any attempt toward guidance, would dismiss my opinion if it didn't match hers. Any comment about her drinking was seen as an attack, which would bring on a tenfold counterattack.

I was just so angry – angry at her drinking, angry at her illness, angry she had given up, angry at her anger, angry at her family for what they had done to her, angry at myself for my inadequacies, my powerlessness, my incapacities. Angry at my anger. Angry at my lack of compassion.

I didn't know what to do, and I was angry that I didn't, angry I'd been put in this position. I sought out Al-Anon, but Laramie is a small town, with a small population. The Al-Anon meetings were small – four of us once or twice, but sometimes only me. I found the meetings unhelpful and stopped going.

I worried about being an enabler. I certainly didn't want to encourage her drinking in any way. But I also had to live with her. Sometimes it was easier to just give in. Easier to survive. We tried several agreements. Or I tried them. She would agree – until she wouldn't.

Riding the motorcycle back from Fort Collins one day, Polly kept sagging off the back. Afraid she would pull us both over, I propped her up with one hand while handling the bike with the other. We stopped and I managed to get us both off the bike without tipping us over. After a while she steadied and we set off again. She started sagging off a second time. Again I managed to get us stopped safely. I was alarmed. I didn't know what was going on with her and didn't know how we could make it back to Laramie. We were in open land and I couldn't leave her on the side of the road. The third time she started drooping off her seat, I managed to stop at a little wayside church that is halfway between Fort Collins and Laramie. I got Polly off the bike and into the church and told her to wait there until I could come back with the car. The whole incident scared us both. After that, I wouldn't let her on the bike. She loved to ride and resented me for my refusal. But she still had enough sense to know that she might kill us both if she couldn't keep herself on the bike.

One day while we were eating lunch together in town she stopped talking and her eyes turned glassy. I realized she wasn't breathing and tried to give her the Heimlich maneuver. Another patron called 911. The medics came and extracted a wad of meat from deep in her throat and revived her. Polly hadn't been breathing for about five minutes – fortunately the firehouse was close-by. They took her to the ER and I called Sarah to sit with me while we waited to see if Polly would be all right. Having been without oxygen for so long, she might have suffered brain damage. Once Polly stabilized, they admitted her to dry her out. After a few days I picked her up, and on the way home she insisted we stop to pick up a bottle of wine.

Another time when we were downtown, she wanted to stop for a drink but I refused to spend the afternoon in a bar. I left her there, but an hour later I got a call from one of the guys at the bar to come get her. It took two of us to get her out to the street and into the car. OK, I thought, we wouldn't do that again.

I wouldn't buy her wine anymore. If she wanted some she'd have to get it herself. After watching her back out of the garage into the neighbor's truck parked across the street, then drive off only to return and bounce the car off the garage before, unconcerned, she managed to get it through the door on the second try, I told her she couldn't drive anymore.

But there was a liquor store she could walk to three blocks away. After a neighbor brought her home I told her I'd get wine if I was out but wouldn't make a special trip.

And so it went. She could always tap into a much deeper well of anger than I could. And after 20 years of marriage, she knew which buttons to push to upset me.

At some point I became determined to survive this ordeal. The oncologist said without treatment she would be dead in five to ten years. I thought: I can do that. I can outlast her.

Years before I had known a nice, kind, sparkly woman whose husband had died in her arms on the dance floor. She had managed to put her life back in order. She fell in love again. He wooed her and took her dancing, but soon after they were married he contracted a disabling disease. For years he was wheelchair-bound and she cared for him. After he died, she began trying to move on again. But soon – too soon – as she was preparing to go out, she collapsed and died. Afraid this would happen to me, I became determined to take care of myself. I would see friends when I could. I would be careful what I ate. I would get some exercise. And I would carve out, somehow, some time for myself.

As Polly's physical and mental health declined, I had less and less time to myself. I began getting up early to walk while it was still dark, to relieve the stress of caring for her, to keep myself moderately healthy, and to give me some time just for myself. I would walk as the day dawned, while the city was still quiet, while I still had some peace before Polly woke up. My walks gave me the strength to make it through one more day.

I couldn't dress up in front of Polly anymore, and I wanted to keep the sanctuary of my dressing separate from my care of her. I began using my early morning time to dress, at least a little. I had to wear pants when I went out, but I could wear other things as long as I was careful – careful to appear normal. I would put on a few things under my coat to give myself the comfort of being just a little bit female.

But gradually I wanted more, needed more. As I dared more I became scared – scared I was losing control, scared of exposure, scared of rejection, scared of losing my position in the neighborhood and town – a position of acceptance that I needed to make it through. I couldn't let whatever was driving me to dress in women's clothes take me over and ruin my life. My life was already precarious. I needed the support of others to make it through the day, sometimes just to make it hour to hour. I couldn't let these inner urges make me do something that would lose that support.

As Polly's disease progressed, she became manipulative and erratic. My understanding was that as her liver failed it couldn't clean the toxins out of her blood and they began to cross the blood/brain barrier, affecting her personality. But at other times she was still the woman I had loved.

Polly resented that my relationship with my daughter was so good. She had wished for that closeness with her father but it had never been possible. As her condition got worse and she needed more care, her resentment increased and she became more bitter and more difficult. Wanting to hurt me and wanting to damage my relationship with Casey, Polly threatened to tell her about my crossdressing, letting her know that her wonderful father wasn't so wonderful after all.

But I wouldn't be pushed that way. Throughout much of my career I'd had security clearances, some of which were of a high level. I justified holding the clearances despite my secret crossdressing by knowing that I would never submit to blackmail. Rather than betray my clearances – rather than tell secrets I didn't know – I would rather stand at the gate of a base with a sign outing myself.

So after Polly threatened to out me, I called Casey. We had a long conversation during which I tried to explain what I still didn't understand myself. I didn't mention Polly's threat. Casey, bless her, was sympathetic and fully supportive. She seemed glad for me to share such an intimate part of myself with her. Her loving acceptance meant a lot to me. And it still does.

The next time Casey visited, I showed her a picture of me dressed in women's clothes. "Oh," she said with some surprise, "It's age-appropriate." At first this seemed like a strange reaction to me, but then I realized the basis for her comment. I know that some crossdressers get stuck at an age or in an era. A fifty-something male-bodied person might dress as a teenage girl – I might have gotten stuck in the era of poodle skirts and bobby sox. I think what happens is the person has trouble progressing beyond where they got blocked in their development as a woman, usually when they found they were having the wrong puberty.

For several years I had been sleeping on a daybed in another room. One night I woke to find that Polly had a nosebleed. I tried to get it stopped but couldn't. I got her out of bed and was guiding her into the bathroom, walking backward in front of her, holding both her hands. She sneezed. A fine mist of blood covered me, the floor, the walls. I slept without clothes during that time, so the bloody mist was on my chest, my stomach, my arms, my legs and feet. Crap! Hepatitis C is a blood-borne disease and now I was covered in it.

I couldn't control her bleeding so I called 911. I quickly cleaned myself and put on some clothes while waiting for them to arrive. The EMT's couldn't control the bleeding either, so they took her to the hospital. They managed to get the bleeding stopped and admitted her to dry her out. To dry her out once again. I returned home about 3 AM and scrubbed the bathroom walls and floor and sink and tub, showered thoroughly, made a mental note to be checked for hep-C once this was over, and collapsed into my bed.

By January of 2007 I was getting to the end of my rope. Polly continued to deteriorate and continued to become more difficult. I could leave her for my walks in the morning while she slept, and I could leave her long enough for a quick trip to the grocery store, but I dared not leave her longer than that. I had found her on the floor at the bottom of the basement stairs one day. Evidently she had tumbled down them. She wasn't hurt, but she couldn't get up and couldn't climb the stairs without help. Another time she called the police when I was in another room – to report my maltreatment of her. Friends who had stayed with her for an hour or two so that I could meet another friend for lunch or to run errands began refusing to stay with her. She'd mess with their minds, so they stayed away. I asked our doctor to OK her for hospice care but he was reluctant, perhaps seeing it as a failure on his part. But finally I convinced him and began getting some help. In-home hospice saved my life.

Polly died in May, the day before our 22nd wedding anniversary. I had checked on her in the middle of the night. She was moaning, evidently in pain. I gave her some morphine to take the edge off and went back to my bed. When I woke at my usual time – between five and six – she was dead. I stood there looking at her and cried. She had been so full of life and now she was dead. We had had sixteen or seventeen good years together, which I figured was a pretty good average.

9

RECOVERING ❋ 2007-2008

"The question is not how to get cured, but how to live."
— Joseph Conrad

It's hard to watch someone die – especially someone you've been close to. I felt so inadequate, so helpless. I felt there was nothing I could do but watch. And ease it as best I could for her. She was helpless, too, in her addiction and her disease and her feeling of futility. It was all so sad, so very sad. And so enervating.

That morning, needing time for myself, needing to get away, I went for my usual morning walk. I called the hospice nurse when I got home. She came and arranged for the mortuary to pick up Polly's body. When the men had arranged Polly on the bed, the nurse asked if I wanted to go in to see her one last time, to say goodbye. But I couldn't. I was a mere simulacrum of myself, hollowed out, hanging on by a thread. I'd been saying goodbye for years and couldn't manage any more.

I called a friend who would pass on the news to everyone else. The neighbors would have seen the mortuary car. I called Casey. I called my sister and relied on her to call my brother. And then I began putting the house in order. I threw out any alcohol I could find. I took her mattress and bedding to the dump. I went through all her clothes, throwing out most of them as unusable and filling six grocery bags with usable items for the thrift store – the little one run by the Episcopal church. There were a few clothes that were still usable that I threw out – they were too distinctively Polly's, and I didn't want to see them walking around Laramie.

I talked to my minister about a memorial service. I wrote an obituary and took it to the newspaper. When it came out, I mailed a copy to one of Polly's aunts in Rhode Island. Polly was the last of her branch of the family, but the aunt would tell the rest of the extended family. The only thing Polly wanted to go to her family was a carved chest an uncle had gotten in Singapore when he was a merchant seaman in the 1930s. I contacted the cousin and had the moving company crate it for shipment.

There was a lot of paperwork to do. I called my broker and went to the bank. As I went through the house, I put things I didn't want to deal with in the basement. Eventually the basement was full. It was a year later before I had the energy to go through what was down there.

I met a friend for lunch or for coffee, always just one friend at a time. I talked to people on the phone, especially including Casey. I was exhausted.

And gradually, slowly, determinedly I began to establish a life for myself.

I blamed Polly and her drinking for the misery of the last few years. And I blamed myself for my inadequacies in helping her. I was sad that she had not been able to pull herself together and sad that she was gone. But I was relieved to be done with the increasingly difficult task of caring for her, of dealing with her, of navigating an almost-impossible passage. And I felt guilty for my relief.

I tried to make sense of it all. Would it have been different if I'd been more understanding, more compassionate? What if I'd done this or that, or hadn't done that or this? Should I have...? But I did the best I could with my abilities at the time. And I have to be gentle with myself for surviving when she didn't, for not doing more, for not being more capable, for not being another person. During those years I learned about who I am, some of which I would be happier not knowing. Watching Polly die and caring for her as she did was the hardest thing I've ever done. I hope I never have to do anything more difficult.

Released from my care-giving duties, I began looking forward to what was next, come what may. I re-established contact with Gretchen, my childhood friend I thought of as my unofficial sister. We had gone our separate ways but still felt the closeness of siblings. When I visited her later that year, I told her that I was entering Phase 5 of my life – the next one after childhood & teens, college & Army, Valerie, Polly.

I continued the counseling I had sought to deal with Polly as she declined physically and her behavior deteriorated. After she died, it became grief counseling. I kept taking the anti-depressants my counselor had prescribed for me even though I didn't like what they did to me – kind of dulled me down. I took them for a few more months, until I felt strong enough to stop them. After about a year, the counseling sessions seemed to have taken me as far as they could and I ended them. I learned to live alone again. And being alone, like when I left Valerie in '83, I began dressing again.

By the fall of '08, fifteen months after Polly's death, I was still struggling. I was still wrestling with my memories, trying to remember the good times and put the awful times in perspective. My anger at her for the misery of those last years had abated, and I was learning to accept my inadequacies as her illness and death companion. I thought I had adjusted to my new life, but I couldn't seem to move on. There was something I needed to take care of – I just didn't know what that was.

Feeling untethered and without direction, I began spending more and more time in women's clothes. I wasn't sure if dressing made me feel vulnerable or if I dressed because I felt vulnerable. The comfort I found wearing a dress and heels made no sense to me, and I'd always wanted things to make sense.

From the times of dressing up in Albert's basement, I had the idea that clothes make the woman. It seemed that dressing up was the only way I could be a woman, even if that was just for a little while. In some ways, I had always thought of wearing women's clothes as just something I did, like a hobby. I was the same person in women's clothes as in men's clothes, just more comfortable, more settled.

Through our lives we have different roles, different aspects of the one person we are. I had been a child, a student, a soldier, a husband. At this time I was a father, a widower, a retiree, a veteran – different aspects of me but all the same me.

As I dressed more and more often in women's clothes I began to feel there was another "me" emerging. This other "me" was part of who I was – I was still one person – but this part of me began taking on a life of its own. At times, I felt like there were two of me – the constrained male me who followed, pretty much, society's expectations, and the freer, relaxed female me who could be more open and friendly. Giving this emerging me a name, I began to think of my women's clothes as Katherine clothes. (Not Katherine's clothes – they were my clothes.)

I don't know where the name Katherine came from. I had an Aunt Catherine I'd met only once and didn't know. Back in my pen pal days, I'd been Betty, but I'd found it difficult for me to enunciate clearly when introducing myself in person. Besides, the alliteration and rhythm in Betty Birdsall didn't set the image I was trying for.

I wanted a woman's name. Not being particularly feminine in appearance, I wanted a name that was clearly female. I didn't want it to be cutesy – I had no desire to even attempt cutesy. Mainly, I wanted a name appropriate for someone my age and background.

My parents had named me Daniel. I was Danny when I was small, but in middle school I had changed it to Dan. Everyone made the shift except my mother, who would still lapse into Danny sometimes, even when I was middle-aged. Daniel (Danny, Dan) was a name I never liked. It was too soft. If I had to be a boy, I wanted a strong name – Spike or Crash or something. But I had been a quiet, shy child and probably would have found a strong name to be a burden. It had been hard enough being Danny.

Although I would have been named Elizabeth if I'd been born with a girl's body, I couldn't picture the person I'd become as Eliza, Liz, Lisa, Liza, Lib, Beth, Betty, or Betsy. Besides, my daughter's middle name was Elizabeth, and adopting that as my own name would be just too weird. Somewhere along the way I had begun to think of this other aspect of me as Katherine.

That fall, as the weather got worse and the days shorter, I spent more time alone, inside my house. On some days, I would dress in Katherine clothes all day except for short excursions out. But sometimes, in the early morning, I wouldn't change when I went out. I began going out more and more in the early morning dark, even shoveling snow off the church sidewalks several times while in my Katherine clothes under my heavy, un-gendered coat in the morning quiet. My increasing boldness scared me, but it somehow fulfilled, partially, a need. I knew something was struggling to get out; I just wasn't sure what that something was.

As sad and difficult as it had been, Polly's death had freed me to work on myself. I thought that maybe while I was waiting to figure out what to do with the rest of my life – what Phase 5 would be – I could deal with what I thought of as my gender issues. I was 65 years old and, as they say, not getting any younger. Actually, aside from my age I was in a good position. Other than internal-izing society's messages, the biggest impediments to exploring one's gender usually are a spouse, a family, and an employer. I was retired and had no spouse or parents, my siblings weren't that close, and even though losing my daughter would be devastating to me, she was a grown woman and would be OK. It seemed to be now or never. And if it was never, I would always wonder what might have been. And the wondering, I knew, would be really hard.

I talked to Penny, my minister, and restarted counseling with Judith, the psychologist who'd helped me so much through Polly's decline and death and the aftermath. I don't remember that Judith told me to do anything, and she didn't give me homework, but it was nice to be able to talk at least about my confusion and my ambivalence and these urges that I couldn't explain. I didn't think I was a crossdresser, despite my need for and pleasure in wearing women's clothes. Or I wasn't *just* a crossdresser.

I never thought of myself as a woman trapped in a man's body, which seemed to be a requirement for being transsexual. I was just whatever I was in my own body. Dressing was a need, but I didn't think it was a fetish. Or perhaps not *just* a fetish. I was some kind of transgender, but what kind?

10

ACKNOWLEDGING ✳ 2008-2009

"My fears teach me courage. My weaknesses couch me to strength. My scars remind me not to make the same mistakes. I can become who I long to be by loving who I am now."
— Toni Sorenson

The bathroom in my Laramie home was small, with just the basics: toilet, pedestal sink, tub/shower combination, and just enough room to move around. It had only one window – a small one of glass brick that couldn't be opened. I'd painted the walls and ceiling a soothing green and installed an exhaust fan to pull out the inevitable moisture. It was a cozy place.

Several years ago, curious how my legs would feel and look in stockings if they were smooth, I had soaked in the tub and carefully scraped away my leg hair. It became a regular thing during the winters – soaking in the tub in my cozy bathroom while winter winds howled outside, scraping away my leg hair. I let the hair grow back when the weather warmed so that I could have hairy legs if I wanted to wear shorts, but come September, when the temperatures dropped and the winds built up, I would again begin shaving my legs. It was wonderfully self-indulgent.

In January of 2009 I began wondering about shaving my face, too. I'd grown a mustache in the Army to annoy the careerists, and I'd worn a full beard since joining the Coast Guard in the early 70s, when sailors could have beards. I'd shaved the beard in the 80s when the rules changed, but I'd grown it back in the 90s when I retired from the service. I'd managed to keep the mustache for forty years – in my mind a minor accomplishment – and my daughter and her mother had never seen me without it.

Somehow my crossdressing and hairy face didn't bother me. It was always easy for me to see myself in the mirror, dressed in a skirt and heels with a silky blouse covering my fake breasts, and with my face hidden by a full beard. I didn't think I'd ever look like a woman anyway, and somehow the clothes and the beard were just part of who I was. But that January I began to think about shaving it all off. I enjoyed the feel of my hairless legs. Perhaps a hairless face would feel good, too.

I gathered what I would need – scissors, razor, shaving soap and brush – and arranged it on the back of the sink. I draped a towel over the sink to catch the whiskers, and began snipping away. Once I started, I would have to continue because the beard would be too patchy if I stopped, but I was calm, curious, not at all anxious. This was just something I was going to do. If I didn't like it, I could grow it all back.

I didn't know it at the time, but I was starting on a path of fear and joy, excitement and worry, confusion and doubt, and, eventually, a growing sense of certainty. But in my cozy bathroom, looking at myself in the mirror over the sink, I knew only that if I was going to continue to live, I needed to be more open – with myself and with the world – and revealing my face was part of that.

Working away, I'd grab a bunch of hair and snip as closely to the skin as I could, then grab another bunch. I worked calmly, methodically. I was in no hurry. Once I'd gotten as much as I could with the scissors, I wrapped up the hair in the towel and began with the razor. I worked carefully and didn't cut myself.

I looked different. I liked the feel of the smooth skin, both to my touch and from the inside, with the air touching it. But I wasn't sure I liked the look. I'd developed a style in Laramie that went with a full beard, and this look was different. I didn't know that I liked seeing my face. Before I'd begun, I'd promised myself that I could grow it all back but that I'd wait two weeks before deciding – two weeks for me to get used to it and to give it a good try. I cleaned up the bathroom and put everything away, shook the towel outside and put it in the laundry, and went about my day.

To me, I looked very different, but no one remarked on my now-clean face. Everyone who recognized me before still recognized me. Perhaps I wasn't that different. A couple of weeks after shaving off the full beard and mustache, an acquaintance asked if I'd gotten new glasses. I looked different but was very much the same.

But I liked having the bare face and didn't even mind too much the need to scrape it clean each morning. I sensed a change, a loosening, but didn't know where I would go with it. When I wrote my friends Mark and Bob in Maryland that I'd shaved and now had a clean face, they wrote back that they knew Polly always liked men with beards, but they preferred women without them.

I struggled to figure out where I fit in the world. I'd always wanted to be a girl and a woman, but I'd lived my life as a boy and man. I had a male skeleton, male genitals, male whiskers, male voice, male upbringing. My life experiences, including my work experiences, were strongly colored by the fact that everyone saw me as a man.

Crossdressing was my refuge, my sanctuary. Would I be happy as an open crossdresser? I didn't know that I had the chutzpah to carry it off. How about if I just presented myself as androgynous? That could be as dangerous and problematic as crossdressing. And besides not being sure that I could carry it off, I really found a lot of comfort having breasts, even if they were artificial. What was that about?

I thought I was stuck with my genitals. I was used to them, after all. Having them didn't bother me, usually. But there had been a few times I'd wanted to slice it all off. I'd wonder how to do it. Perhaps a set of bolt cutters would work. It'd have to be quick and decisive. Would I have to sharpen the blades? And sterilize them somehow? I wouldn't want to get blood poisoning. And if I did manage it, how would I stop the bleeding? There's probably a good blood supply to that area. I'd probably pass out and bleed to death before coming to, and what's the point in that? The idea was to live without the extra baggage. Nope. The whole idea wasn't practical, so I'd put it away along with everything else I didn't want to look at too closely.

I didn't think about it often, but it worried me. I could feel myself edging closer to what I thought of as passive suicide – doing increasingly risky things that at some point one of them would kill me. I needed help, and that's why I'd begun talking about my gender issues with Judith, my counselor, and Penny, my minister. It was why I needed to tell my friends, needed to be more open, needed to come to terms with these strange feelings. I needed to understand them.

I'd managed to keep it all inside for so many years, but I felt I wouldn't be able to much longer. The problem that was trying to kill me wasn't the genitals, it was keeping the secret, keeping it all inside. I needed to let it out and deal with the consequences. Instead of worrying about how to sterilize bolt cutters, I needed to think how best to rid myself of this secret that was festering inside me.

I wanted to talk to people who had already been down this

path. There was no Renaissance chapter anywhere near. I wrote the office in Pennsylvania but never heard back. Although I wasn't sure I would fit in their group, I tried to connect with the Denver chapter of Tri-Ess, a longstanding national organization of male crossdressers, but no one replied.

During one of my frequent trips to Fort Collins, Colorado, on an unfamiliar back street near downtown, I saw a storefront with a rainbow flag and a bunch of posters. Curious, I walked up and looked in the windows. The office was closed, but it appeared to be a community organization supporting LGBT people – Eclectic. Back home, I found their website and emailed them for more information. Someone wrote back, inviting me to their trans-gender support group that met once a month. I decided to go to the next meeting some weeks later despite it being in the evening and 65 miles away.

I wondered why I wanted to come out, why I wanted to go to the support group, why I wanted to open this door. I was doing well living as a man, even if in private I dressed as a woman. I wasn't going to transition to living as a woman. I wasn't going to have my penis removed. I was just searching to understand what I was, unsure where all this was going.

The first Eclectic meeting was small – four of us including Maria, a young trans woman who led the group. We were an assortment of ages and stages. I was pleased when Maria told me I would be able to pass as a woman because I didn't send out a lot of male vibes. She gave me hope. Perhaps it wasn't just outward appearance – clothes and makeup and hair. And perhaps presenting myself as a woman might be possible. Difficult, scary, uncertain maybe, but perhaps not impossible.

When I was a child living with my family, we had an unabridged dictionary always open on a table. If one of us kids asked what something meant, we were told to look it up. And of course often the definition would require us to look up a few more words, which might require more research.

In Laramie, I was looking up something in Wikipedia that led me to something that led me to the term "genderqueer." I read the definition with growing surprise. I had sometimes thought that I was, somehow, at the same time both male and female and neither. This term seemed to fit me perfectly. Wow. Here, in digital print was a word that fit me. Surely the term hadn't been coined just for me. Even though I always somehow knew I wasn't unique in my gender confusion, here was confirmation that there were others like me. I might be a subset of a subset, but I wasn't alone. Finding this word in Wikipedia was, for me, an epiphany.

(Now, years later, I don't think that I'm genderqueer. My understanding of myself and of the range of gender nonconformance has grown. But at the time, the word was meaningful to me as no other term had been. It was a validation from the world at large.)

Back in the 90s, I'd bought the book *Outing Yourself* by Michelangelo Signorile. It was addressed mainly to gay men but was certainly applicable for lesbians. I had read some of it, but it didn't seem applicable to me. I hadn't been ready to use it then. I still had the book and began reading it again. With some translation, it worked for someone like me, whose problem was identity rather than orientation.

The book has a series of exercises, the first few of which are to learn to accept yourself as you are – gay, lesbian, transgender – and how you are seen by some – fag, dyke, whatever. I worked through the exercises until I got to the parts about coming out at work and coming out to your parents. I was retired and my parents were long gone. I felt like I'd gotten what I could from the book.

I edged closer to coming out as a crossdresser. I had talked to my minister and counselor about my crossdressing. My daughter and my gay friends on the East Coast knew I wore women's clothes. But I needed to come out to my Laramie friends. I was tired of the hiding. This had been a part of me since I was little. It was time to stop denying I was this way. This secret I'd kept for over 60 years was getting harder and harder to keep. I almost told a woman I barely knew. I was close to blurting it out, regardless of the circumstances or to whom. But the crux of what I gleaned from *Outing Yourself* was to control the process as best I could.

My plan, if all went well, was to make a lunch or coffee date with each of my closest friends. I wanted to tell them individually but in rapid succession. I didn't want them to have to keep my secret from each other. If worse came to worst, I could always move away. I was well-integrated into Laramie and was enjoying more friendships than I'd ever had, but the only person whose rejection would truly deeply wound me was my daughter's. Other than that possibility, what did I have to lose?

Even though I was preparing to spring myself on my friends, the town, and perhaps the outside world, I was going to do it cautiously. I knew that once the door was open, it couldn't be shut again. The secret couldn't be untold. I thought that perhaps if it all went badly, I could start fresh somewhere else. But I was also slowly becoming aware that, for me, for my well-being, I would have trouble cramming myself back into the closet after opening the door once. So perhaps the door was opening irreversibly, and out I'd come. But who would be there, blinking in the unaccustomed light, revealed at last? Revealed, that is, to me as well as to everyone else.

I thought I would start with Bruce, a single man about my age who had become a good friend. We met each week for lunch at a Chinese buffet, and sometimes we joked that the family who ran the place might think we were partners. But I ended up first telling Jim, a married man also about my age. He had been trained as a priest in some version of Eastern Orthodox Catholicism before deciding that kind of life wasn't for him. We saw each other often, but our only standing date was for a long, chatty lunch before our monthly volunteer chore of cleaning the church together. And that date was to be the day after I decided I was ready to begin telling my secret.

It was a beautiful Laramie morning – sunny and clear, with temperatures in the 20s and the usual 10-15 mph wind. I was excited and a little anxious, and I think a little numb. Jim's friendship meant a lot to me. He was my local "in case of emergency" contact. He had a key to my house and access to my safety deposit box at the bank. I trusted him completely. He was very accepting and open-minded, but this might be too odd even for him.

We met at our usual lunch place – a sandwich shop that looked like it may have been built originally as part of a long-defunct chain of Mexican restaurants, along a main street among the car lots and fast-food places. There was a drive-through window, half a dozen low-backed booths and a few more tables inside, and a patio with more tables, now closed for the long winter.

It was a place where workers and a few students grabbed lunch in the middle of a busy day. We stood in line to order at the counter and waited while the young woman cashier got our sodas and loaded our trays with our sandwiches. Jim and I often ordered the same thing, but I always got potato chips and he liked French fries.

We tossed our coats onto the benches of a booth and settled in, facing each other across the red laminate table. I had been tense earlier, but I always enjoyed being with Jim, and I relaxed into our usual easy conversation. We talked about Laramie and the people we both knew. Jim updated me about his son and daughter-in-law in New York. We talked about the church and about the university. Jim ate there more often than I did, and he greeted the shop's owner when he came by. We continued to sit there, nursing our drinks, our food long gone, chatting comfortably as the lunch crowd left.

I wanted to come out to Jim, but I wanted to enjoy our time together first. And I wanted to wait until after our visit, so he could leave if he wanted to. I didn't know how he would take my announcement, and I wanted to hold onto this normalcy of our being together as long as I could.

Finally we wound down and began to think about going to clean the church. I knew I had to tell him now. I said, "Before we go, I want to tell you something about myself. I'm transgender, and I've worn women's clothes now and then all of my life."

Silence. He sat there, stunned, trying to think of what to say.

I waited for him to process my announcement, and then I said, "I don't know what I'm going to do, but I need to be more open about it and wanted to tell you myself. I didn't want you to find out indirectly."

That seemed to help him. He said, "OK, let's go clean the church," and we went out to our separate cars.

At the church, we settled into our usual routine. It was my turn to vacuum and straighten, his turn to clean the kitchenette and rest rooms. I worked away, relieved that I had managed to tell Jim and happy to have a normal, mundane task to do.

We worked separately for about an hour. When we'd put away the vacuum and cleaning supplies and had bagged up the trash, we locked up and walked to our cars in the lot. Jim said, "I'm the same and you're the same. Please keep me up to date as you go forward." I thanked him, waved good-bye, and drove home.

So it had begun. I had cracked open the door. After so many years of safety, I had set off on a path that led I knew not where. But now that I had started, I had to keep going. It was a relief.

Not wanting Jim to have to keep my secret from his wife, I called her and set up a coffee date for the next morning.

I met Marian at the coffee shop downtown that we both liked. We chatted easily for a while, and when I judged enough time had gone by, I told her I was transgender. She asked a couple of questions and then, losing interest, asked what trips I had planned for the summer. I began to realize that being transgender – a secret I'd guarded for all these years – might be far more interesting to me than to anyone else.

Feeling good about how this was going, I met with and told ten more friends. One was Catie, who had worked in grief counseling and had been a resource for me after Polly's death. During my coffee date with her, I went through my by-now practiced routine, visiting with her before making my announcement. But when I told her that I was transgender, without hesitation she replied, "I know." She threw me off my stride with that one. Unfortunately, I was so focused on my script that I didn't think to ask how she had come to that conclusion.

As I told more friends, I felt lighter and lighter, as if a weight that had pressed me down most of my life was gradually being lifted. Everyone I told accepted what I said and accepted me as I was. Their reactions ranged from Jim's initially being stunned to Marian's disinterest to Catie's "I know."

I worried about telling Bill, my weekly coffee date. He was eighteen years older, wore two hearing aids, and relied to some extent on reading lips, which had become more difficult for him as his macular degeneration progressed. We met in a busy and sometimes noisy coffee shop. I didn't want to have to shout my announcement to him. And, with our age difference, I thought he might be more resistant to my trying to escape gender norms. I had thought about skipping him in my series of announcements but decided I valued his friendship too much to do that.

As it turned out, I didn't have to raise my voice. He listened intently – one of his traits that I really appreciated. When I said I didn't know if I would do anything about being transgender other than telling my friends, he asked me: "How long do you have left? Thirty years?" I was 65. "Well, maybe 20," I replied. And he said, "That's a long time to be unhappy." Bless you, Bill.

Another of Bill's wonderful traits was his curiosity. At each of our coffee dates over the next few months, he always wanted to hear about my latest steps and encounters on this adventure I was undertaking.

By telling my friends, I had opened a door to free myself. I wanted to be more open – more open with them and more open with myself. I didn't realize it at the time, but I had set in motion a process I could guide but not control, a process that swept me along with all my friends and everyone I knew into an unknown future.

Now that I'd told my friends, I wanted to try leaving the house as a woman. I had gone to the Renaissance dinner in Pennsylvania ten years earlier, but that had been my only experience in public. I learned that Wyoming Equality, the state-wide LGBT group, was having a game night and dance in Cheyenne. This seemed like an opportunity for me to dress up away from people I knew. I contacted the group to find out if I would be welcome. They assured me I would. I told my friends I was going, to try it out.

I didn't want to have to drive the hour back to Laramie late at night, so I reserved a motel room in Cheyenne. I packed carefully. I wanted to look as good as I could, given my limitations. I had never worn a wig and up to that time had never tried makeup. I just wanted to be me, with breasts and dressed in a skirt and heels.

On the day of the dance I drove over to Cheyenne and checked into the motel. I must have eaten supper, but I have no memory of it. I dressed carefully in my room: sheer stockings on my freshly shaved legs, the foam "breast enhancers" in a bra to give me a little shape, a white half-slip so my skirt wouldn't cling to my legs, and a black pencil skirt. I had learned that I needed a skirt with a structured waist, so I would have at least the appearance of hips. And I liked the feminine touch of a white, lace-trimmed half-slip under it. I put on a mock-neck shirt to keep me warm in the Wyoming winter, black to match the skirt, hoping to deemphasize my long torso and unfeminine shoulders. I cinched a wide black belt around my waist. I would never have an hourglass figure, but having something of a waist helped. Earrings, necklace, bracelet. I wore no makeup, relying on the clothes to help me look and feel like a woman.

I stepped into my three-inch heels and looked in the room's full-length mirror. To me I looked good, but I had learned I wasn't the best judge of that. Regardless, I felt great. It was quite an adventure to get dressed up in an anonymous motel room, putting on what had always been forbidden and private.

I loaded my wallet and keys into my purse and added a small digital camera. I wanted a record of this excursion if I could summon the courage to ask someone to take my picture. I put on a scarf and a woman's black peacoat, checked my hair one last time, and pulled on gloves. I was ready – nervous, excited, and ready.

I ducked out a side door to avoid the motel lobby. I might be ready to premiere at an LGBT gathering, but I wasn't yet ready to walk out into the straight world. Very carefully, I drove to the dance. My car had a manual transmission and this was the first time I'd driven in heels. I didn't want to scuff the shoes on the pedals. And dressed as I was, I certainly didn't want to be in a crash and have to stand on the side of the road waiting for the police to show up. Besides, it was very cold out, and I was dressed for looks, not weather.

The dance was in an event room in the basement of the airport. The Cheyenne, Wyoming, airport is not large. I parked next to the terminal and sat in the car for a few minutes, screwing up my courage. I knew I had to go in. I would be really disappointed in myself if I had gotten this far – Cheyenne, the motel, dressing up, and driving here – if I didn't go in. Finally, I said, "Show time!" and stepped out.

Walking through the ice in the parking lot, in the dark and in heels, was a challenge, but at least I was alone.

Nervous, apprehensive, determined, I walked into the warm, brightly lit terminal. For better or worse, Katherine was here at the Cheyenne airport.

Besides the few boarding gates in the terminal, there was a restaurant and maybe a shop or two, but they were closed. Scheduled flights were few. As luck would have it, though, one had just arrived and there were more people there than was usual. Most of them were at the other end of the terminal, but the noise of my heels loudly tapping on the terrazzo floor rose above the din. After a short search, I found the stairs down to the dance.

I was immediately welcomed, although many eyes swung to check me out when I entered. I was invited to join a table of gay men about my age playing some inane game that was just an excuse to be together. I relaxed into their company.

By the time I had to go upstairs and down the terrazzo floor to the bathroom, the terminal was empty. I went into the men's room out of habit. It only occurred to me while washing my hands that when sitting in the first stall, my heels and stockinged legs had been visible immediately to anyone entering. But I was alone.

When the game part of the evening ended and the dance began, many of the older crowd left and lots of young people came in. I spent about an hour talking to a woman who was the only other identifiably trans person there. She was an Air Force veteran and talked about her struggles to get the service to accept her new identity. At the time, I wasn't thinking I'd transition. I thought I could be happy having outlets like this evening, when I could dress up and show some of the me I usually kept hidden from the world.

But the next morning at the motel I wanted to go to the diner next door for breakfast. I had enjoyed my evening out as Katherine, but I thought it would be wise to be my male self at the diner in the light of day. It was very hard to pull on my male clothes – the jeans and flannel shirt cut for a male body – cut for my male body. I knew then that I was in trouble. Switching back and forth was going to be much, much harder than I'd thought.

I had been eight or nine when my brother introduced me to science fiction. I didn't like the stories of monsters or fighting. What I loved were stories that were ordinary except for one or two things – ordinary life on Main Street America, except mischievous Martians show up, or a man finds a watch that stops time. Or not Main Street America but a civilization much like ours but different in one way. And that one way affects everything. I wondered at the authors' creativity and imagination.

As a child, my imagination was more limited. In my world, there were men and women, male and female. People were one or the other. The idea that someone could be both, or neither, or move from one category to the other was beyond my imagining. Someone with a penis was male, period. This understanding of the world was so basic it wasn't questioned. It was so very basic that it was below aware thought. And when we don't even realize our assumptions, we can't question them. It is only when we see the frame around the picture that we can begin to wonder what lies outside it. Question your assumptions, they say. But if you can't see them, you can't question them.

In the narrow world of my childhood, things were clear: I had a male body, therefore, ipso facto, I was a boy. I wanted to be a girl. I thought my body might correct itself. But there was no question in my mind that I was a boy. I just needed to accept the fact and try to be happy with my lot in life.

Actually, my lot was pretty darn good. I was healthy, part of an educated, middle-class family that loved each other, of English extraction in a country that valued that. I was reasonably intelligent, of average size, with regular features and no limiting impediments. I had it better than many.

When we are told all of our lives that there are only two possibilities, either/or, it can be hard to look beyond that. Some of us think outside the box, but for many of us the box becomes our world. There is no "outside the box." Perhaps one value of science fantasy writing is in teaching us that other worlds are possible. And perhaps that is why closed societies, closed cultures, closed minds, restrict access to thought experiments, restrict wondering, restrict science and literature and the arts.

I had fallen into the trap. I had a male body and therefore was a man even though I didn't feel I was. I wasn't a woman. Just about everyone who looked at me could see I wasn't. So I must be a man.

Except I wasn't.

Facing no headwind, I told more people about my crossdressing. I'd been uncorked, and what had been bottled up inside me all those years bubbled out. I was so happy to be free of this secret that I was tempted to stop people on the street to tell them I'm transgender. I didn't. I managed to hold onto a *little* restraint.

I thought that if I was going to be believable as a woman, I needed to work on my voice. The testosterone had lowered it years ago and given it the timber of a male. My natural singing voice was baritone. I thought perhaps someone in the university's drama department might help. I made an appointment with the voice coach, who turned out to be my friend Bill's daughter-in-law. After all, Laramie is a small place.

I explained to her what I wanted. We talked about the techniques she teaches her male actors when they are playing women. She talked about flipping up the back of my palate when I spoke, and to form the sounds there rather than down in my throat. I tried over and over until she could tell I had the right idea, but it would take practice. She also said I could raise my voice at the end of each sentence, making each statement into a question. I acknowledged that but never practiced it. I knew she was from the South, and that's a speech pattern I associate with that region. No woman I knew in Wyoming spoke that way.

At one point as we were talking about all this as I practiced, she talked about how dry cleaners charged so much more for women's shirts and jackets than for men's – often twice as much. She concluded with a disgruntled, "Welcome to Woman World." I've thought of her saying that any number of times since then. Yes, Woman World has a lot of drawbacks – even more than I knew at the time – but I still wanted to live in it.

She was very helpful, but she wasn't willing to coach me on an on-going basis. She didn't think her abilities were right to undertake something like that. I went home and practiced flipping my soft palate up and speaking from my mouth instead of my throat. I think I got to a point where I was comfortable speaking as she advised, but the chest resonance is still there. It comes out particularly on the telephone – partly due to the instrument itself but also, I think, because the listener has no visual cues to go with the voice.

I would correct most people on the telephone when they misgendered me. Sometimes it worked and sometimes it worked for just part of the conversation and they soon reverted to "sir." I remember one young woman – or at least the person had the voice of a young woman. When I told her my name was Katherine, she said, "You don't sound like a Katherine." I replied, "Oh yeah, I ruined my voice years ago." She was fine after that. Through the years I've become more successful at being interpreted as a woman on the telephone. I'm not sure why this is so, but I am pleased. Some of it may be because I am settling more and more into the role that is more natural for me.

I began realizing that I wasn't a crossdresser. I seemed to need more than to just wear women's clothes sometimes. It began to look like I was heading toward living as a woman, although that idea was hard for me. I'd managed to keep it all inside me for so many years that I was afraid to look at it too closely. I knew that some people thought my being transgender was a choice I was making, but to me it seemed more as something that had been thrust upon me. How I dealt with it was the choice.

I was proclaiming that I was, at least sometimes, Katherine. I'd told my friends. I'd been to the event in Cheyenne. I'd gotten new glasses with more androgynous frames. I ordered a new license plate for my car that said KATE. I called my bank and asked for checks and a Visa card with Katherine on them. I called the local DMV office and asked for a second driver's license for Katherine. With the Katherine Visa card, I thought a matching driver's license would be good while I was dressed as a woman. The woman at DMV explained that I could have only one license at a time. She also said I couldn't change my gender marker without surgery – even with the new name I would have an "M" on my license. I was impressed that she knew this without looking it up. Evidently I wasn't the first to ask.

I had been building a local support network and hadn't told anyone who wasn't in Laramie. This was where I was living, and this was where I'd need friends if it all blew up in my face. But during one counseling session, while I was bubbling away about telling my friends and about their reactions, Judith, who almost never gave me direction, asked if I had told my daughter. No, I hadn't. Casey was going through a difficult time with her husband, and I certainly didn't want to add to her burdens. But Judith insisted I needed to tell her.

And so I did. Knowing Casey, I expected her to accept what I was doing. What I didn't expect was her enthusiasm for it.

I've always been a bit awkward on the telephone, but as we talked I relaxed into it. Casey took my news as exciting – how wonderful that I was able at last to open up to who I am, what an adventure this would be. She did worry, though, about me doing this in the wilds of Wyoming. But she seemed to relax as I told her about all the acceptance I was getting from my friends. It was an odd conversation at times; a third party listening to it might wonder which of us was the parent and which the child. I was still wavering about how far I was going with this, but she seemed to be several steps ahead of me.

I worried that I'd never actually be a woman – not a real one, anyway. She wasn't concerned, replying, "Simone de Beauvoir wrote over 500 pages on what it is to be a woman and never came up with any firm conclusions."

We chatted on happily, but at one point she reverted to child again, asking worriedly, "Will you still be my father?" Touched deeply, I reassured her, "I will always be your father, Casey." But then there was the problem of what she should call me. "Papa" no longer seemed right, and our language doesn't have a good word for a father who is a woman. I was unhappy for her, putting her in this awkward position, and said I would accept whatever term she felt comfortable with. Over the next year we tried several things before finally settling on "Mama Kate."

We talked for an hour and a half. I was delighted to have this ally, this daughter I had loved all her life. As we said good-bye, she said sweetly, "Oh thank you for giving me something nice to think about." Was it even possible for me to be more fortunate?

During our phone conversation, Casey asked if I'd told my hairdresser. No, I hadn't thought of that. Casey said, "Oh, you have to tell her *first*." I'd wanted to be a girl and woman all of my life, but I had a lot to learn.

I had a hair appointment a few days later. At the time, Susan worked alone in her own salon. When I got there, before I sat in the chair, I said, "Before you pick up anything sharp, I have something to tell you." She was thrilled. She wanted to cut my hair in a more feminine style and convinced me to dye it to cover the gray. It came out pretty dark, so she dyed it again. This time it was kind of orange, but I wasn't willing to let her try again. A few weeks later, my friend Marian told me that wasn't a good color for me. I assured her I'd get it toned down at my next appointment. I'd never dyed my hair before and was worried about damaging it if I got it dyed too often.

I began thinking about having my facial hair removed. I'd worn a beard when I could and a mustache since my Army days, but now I began to think I'd like a permanently clean face. I knew that if I had laser and electrolysis I would never again be able to grow a beard, but I figured I was done with that. One reason I wore a beard was because I disliked shaving, so having the hair removed wasn't a drawback in that way. And I thought that it would help feminize my face, and therefore I would look a little more believable when dressed as a woman.

I found a laser technician in town and went to her. She was polite but gave me several valid-sounding reasons why she wouldn't be able to help me. It was only later that I realized she just didn't want to do it. I wasn't insulted. Actually, I was thankful she had declined. I didn't want to be subjected to an inherently painful procedure week after week by someone who resented having to do it.

Eclectic, the community organization in Fort Collins, had a list of resources for transgender people. These were providers who were familiar with transgender needs and would be welcoming rather than difficult or reluctant. Such a list was very helpful – almost a Yelp for the transgender community. On my next trip to the support group, I looked at the list for a laser tech. I called and made an appointment for a consult the next week.

I'd never worn makeup. Once, when I was about eleven, I'd snuck into my sister's room and used her lipstick. I'd found it so very difficult to get off that I'd never used any since. My friend Catie, who knew I was transgender without my telling her, offered to bring a Mary Kay representative to my house, to teach me how to put on makeup. I had a wide circle of friends, but most of them knew each other. It was kind of a closed system. But Catie always seemed to know people I had no idea lived in Laramie. When

Brenda came, she looked to me more like suburban middle-America than Laramie. How had I never seen her before in town?

I brought an extra chair from the dining room and we three settled around the kitchen table. Brenda had brought two large cases. One looked like an oversized tackle box and the other like something a Fuller Brush salesman would carry. She opened them to reveal the secrets within and proceeded to give me a course in Makeup 101. There was special skin cleaner and toner and lotion and cream. There was powder for the face and colored powder for the cheeks, with different brushes for each. There was a suite of various bottles and powders and pencils and brushes just for the eyes. And lips – not just lipstick but gloss and liner, too. I was eager to learn, but it was a little overwhelming. I was reminded of when I was dating Casey's mother. I had told her how much I liked that she wasn't all made up but looked so natural. She laughed and said it took her an hour each day to achieve that look.

Finally, Brenda got to the point in the process of taking it all off. She stressed the importance of doing that. There was cleanser for the eyes and cleanser for the face. And then cream for the face and a separate one to reduce the puffiness below the eyes. After two hours, the kitchen table was covered with brushes and applicators and makeup and skincare product. With Lou Ann's "Welcome to Woman World" echoing in my mind, I bought the lot. It appeared that living as a woman was going to require a lot more than just putting on a skirt instead of pants.

A few days later, Susan, my hairdresser, decided she'd take me to the MAC store at the Cherry Creek Mall in Denver. It would be more than two hours each way, so it'd be most of the day. She picked me up after breakfast and we set off. I'd dressed carefully in pencil skirt and heels but had left my face bare – a blank canvas for the makeup person to work on. After driving an hour, Susan pulled into a McDonald's alongside the interstate – she needed coffee. I considered staying in the car but I wanted a bathroom break and maybe something to drink. Nervously, I walked into the McDonald's. I half expected everyone to stare, alarm bells to go off, and the clothing police to rush in and cart me away.

Nothing. No one noticed. Actually, I was a little disappointed. I was discovering, yet again, that this whole thing was a far bigger deal for me than for anyone else.

Susan and I continued south. We walked through the mall to a store open on two sides. There, a young man worked on me for an hour, chattering away about the products, how to apply them, and his experience with other transgender customers. He did a good job but of course applied a lot more makeup than I would ever use. I bought the things I thought I might use again.

Susan and I had lunch in a mall restaurant, cruised through Nordstrom's shoe department, used the rather plush mall ladies' room, and drove back to Laramie. It was quite a day.

Things were moving really fast. I still wasn't sure where this was going. I wasn't sure what I wanted. I was taking one step at a time, but quickly. Transitioning to living full time as a woman was beginning to seem surprisingly doable. But I was scared.

One reason I hadn't tried to transition in the 1980s was because I couldn't figure out how to do it. Things were different 25 years later. Now I had the support of my counselor and minister, and the understanding of my friends. But how do you do it? What was the procedure, the mechanism? I needed some advice.

Like one does with any question in the early 21st century, I searched the Internet. You can turn up a lot of really strange stuff if you set your search engine for "transgender" or "transsexual," but eventually I found a few sites that were helpful. The one I found most helpful was Susan's Place[1], with a trove of valuable information and a very active forum.

People were logging in from all over the world. Because every-thing was in English, most participants lived in the US, Britain, or Australia, but people in other places logged in, too. There were plenty of male-to-female and female-to-male and questioning and others. It quickly became clear that there were many others like me. The stories and angst were similar for most of us. There was a lot of help and a little bad advice. In some ways, I was better off than many, but transitioning in a small town and at such a late age presented its own set of challenges. Still, we had much in common.

I began spending more and more time on the site, posting comments, questions, updates. I learned a lot and found it very helpful. Eventually, I was asked to be one of the moderators. The forum was invaluable to me. I got wonderful support from friends and professionals, but it really helped to "talk" with people about issues my friends might not understand, know about, or be interested in.

I was still undecided about how far I wanted to pursue the goal of living as a woman. One problem was that I looked like a man even when dressed as a woman. I'd always been rather angular and thought perhaps hormones would round the edges a bit. I had researched the effects of estrogen enough to know most of what to expect, at least physically. The long list of effects all sounded good to me except for a loss of upper body strength and an increased risk of deep vein thrombosis (DVT). I'd had a DVT 30 years earlier but thought the estrogen was worth the risk. I knew I couldn't go back to living solely as a man.

I went to see my doctor. Kurt and I had worked closely together through the years of Polly's decline and had established a level of mutual respect and regard that I've enjoyed with no other physician. I talked to him about using hormones. He said that he was willing to prescribe them for me but had never done it for a physical male. He asked me to wait two weeks while he looked into it. I also asked him about an orchiectomy – castration. He said he knew of only one doctor qualified to do that in Laramie. He was doubtful that that particular man would do it, but he'd check.

During our conversation, Kurt told me that I was born this way and that there was nothing wrong with me. The medical community still didn't know exactly what happened for someone to be born transgender, but he thought it had to do with washes of hormones at different stages while in the uterus – that the sex identity of our bodies and of our brains happened at different times and so could be subjected to a different hormone mix.

Knowing that the American Psychiatric Association's Diagnostic and Statistical Manual of Mental Disorders (DSM) classed transgender as a disorder, I told him, "I've been successful as a man, so I don't have a disorder." He replied, "But you should have a chance to be happy."

I almost cried. He told me what I had always sensed: I was OK – I was not a freak or a pervert or crazy. Hearing this stated by a medical man I respected and trusted gave me the validation I'd sought but failed to get ten years earlier at the renowned Johns Hopkins Sex and Gender Clinic.

(I read now that the head of the unit, a man I met and thought an ass, has finally been disavowed by Johns Hopkins for his anti-LGBT views.[2] But he managed to use the reputation of Johns Hopkins to run the clinic for 27 years under the belief that homosexuality is an "erroneous desire" and that treating transgender people with surgery is "like performing liposuction on an anorexic child" – that LGBT people could be "healed" only through psychiatry. When presented with parents agonizing over the birth of an inter-sexed baby, he advised them to surgically "correct" the infant, raise the child as the gender they wanted and the child would adapt. There was a very high suicide rate among such infants when they reached adolescence. How he managed to hold the Johns Hopkins management in thrall for all those years I don't know, but it seems he damaged a lot of lives during his tenure.)

The next day I was to meet the Fort Collins laser tech. The office was 72 miles from my home, but it was usually an easy drive across the prairie and over the hills. The business was a step beyond a beauty parlor or day spa. Among other things, it did laser hair removal and had an associated plastic surgeon. Jody, the laser technician, was an energetic 30 year-old of medium height. She was knowledgable, enthusiastic about her chosen field, and appeared confident in her skills. I liked her immediately.

She explained that treatments would be only partially effective but that the laser would be quicker and less painful than electrolysis. I could finish up with electrolysis. She described the feeling of the laser as being like someone snapping a rubber band against my skin. She explained how hair grows and that the treatments were good only on hairs that were in one third of their growing cycle, so even if she could do everything in one session I would need to return twice more at about monthly intervals. She asked if I'd like the first treatment that day. I agreed. And so the long process of hair removal began.

But I kept wondering whether I was on the right track. Should I just continue to crossdress at home? Should I go into town now and then? Should I dress all the time but keep my male body and name? Should I try to become a woman as much as I could? How would I know? I couldn't go back – I'd told too many people.

One day I drove to the shopping mall in Fort Collins dressed as Katherine. I had a wonderful time looking at clothes, getting lunch, talking to sales clerks. It was one more big step – venturing out on my own during the day. It was very freeing. But each time I went out as Katherine it became harder to stuff myself back into being an ersatz man. I began to realize that, for me, transition might be easier than trying to live as a crossdresser.

But I kept vacillating. One day I was sure I wanted to transition, the next I'd be full of doubts. Was I doing this just because I was discovering I could? But it felt right – scary, but right. This would be a big step – a huge step – and at some point it would be something that couldn't be undone. I had a lifetime of thinking I could never be accepted as a woman, yet more and more that is what I wanted, even if it was imperfect, even if it brought problems, even if it shortened the life I had left. I had lived happily in my cage dreaming of being free. But now I was managing to pry open the door. Did I dare to fly out? What would I find there? Would I wish I was back in the familiarity of my cage? Now was my chance, perhaps my only chance.

Around this time, the newspapers were running stories of a murder in nearby Greeley, Colorado. A young woman had been viciously beaten to death by her new boyfriend when he discovered she had a male body. The proximity of this violence to my town was chilling – somehow it's always easier to dismiss things that are farther away. In Greeley, as the trial approached, the murderer offered the "panic defense" – essentially a form of temporary insanity brought on by the sheer horror of discovering the woman you were sexually attracted to has a penis. This defense had worked in other cases when transgender women were killed, with the juries agreeing that such a discovery would be so very shocking and disgusting that murdering the person was an understandable reaction. This case, however, turned out differently, and for the first time the murderer was convicted of a hate crime and sentenced to life in prison plus 60 years. But the running commentary leading up to and during the trial brought home to me just how socially repugnant I was and how dangerous my life could be. Even more than that, I realized, it was the secret itself that could be more dangerous than the fact of being transgender.

By the end of the month I was convinced I wanted to live the rest of my life as a woman, come what may. I wanted estrogen. I wanted a vagina. I wanted to be a woman as much as I could manage. I might be an XY woman, but I would be a woman nonetheless.

I went back to see Kurt, more convinced than ever that I

wanted to live as a woman. He gave me a prescription for hormones and reported, disgustedly, that when he asked the local urologist about me getting an orchiectomy, the urologist had asked, "Why would he want to do that?" I filled the estrogen prescription on the way home and began taking them the next morning.

Hormones are powerful things. They affect almost every aspect of who we are. On my third day on estrogen, it seemed to kick in. I thought, "So this is how I'm supposed to feel." I felt calmer, steadier, more solid and whole. It smoothed me down. It was as if most of my life I'd been coping with ruffled feathers, a prickliness I had to fight to control, an alien presence within me. The estrogen settled me. Somehow I knew this – this feeling throughout my system – was where I needed to be. It just felt right. The deep feeling of "rightness" I got from the estrogen was just another step – a big one – that let me know I was on the right track.

(I was talking with a transgender man a few months ago. He told me about getting on testosterone after years of his body producing estrogen. I said that testosterone always made me edgy but estrogen had smoothed me out. He said his experience was the opposite – testosterone smoothed him out after years of estrogen-induced edginess. Evidently our systems know what are the right hormones, regardless of which ones our bodies produce.)

For weeks I had been trying to write letters to my sister, my brother, and Gretchen. I didn't know what to say – much of the time I didn't know where this was all going. I'd written about being transgender and needing to explore what that meant to me, but I hadn't mailed the letters. It was a major step. Telling one more friend in Laramie about the new me was no big deal. But telling my sister, my brother, and my unofficial sister, Gretchen, somehow seemed like one more nail in the coffin of the old me.

When I finally did write, my sister and brother accepted the change reluctantly, not really understanding my need and worried about me taking this perilous path. But Gretchen wrote back happily, writing that she'd always had an almost-brother and now she had an almost-sister. She also wrote: "Well, now we know what Phase 5 will look like."

11

REVEALING ✳ 2009

"Integrity is telling myself the truth. And honesty is telling the truth to other people."
— Spencer Johnson

My next big step to release myself from the cage I'd lived in for so long was to come out to my church. I had told my friends, my doctor, my minister, my counselor, my daughter and my siblings, but there were many others I needed to tell before I went much further.

After Polly and I had moved to Laramie in December, 2001, we had begun attending the Unitarian Universalist Fellowship and soon became deeply involved. By the following June I was treasurer and on the board of directors. Seven years later, I was still treasurer and on the board. I cleaned the building once a month with Jim, did repairs with Steve, shoveled the sidewalks in winter, and otherwise made myself useful. I knew each of the 50+ members and all of the regular visitors. My friends were current and former members of the church. The church had given me purpose in retirement and support during Polly's descent into death. It was integral to my life in Laramie.

I had been talking to Penny, the minister, since the beginning of the year, keeping her apprised of my progress and relying on her support. I began talking to her about coming out to the church. At some point as I was talking about coming out to people, she said that I'd never come out to her. Taken aback, I said, "But Polly told me she'd told you that I crossdressed." Penny replied, "She told me a lot of things. I never knew what to believe."

Our Sunday services included a period we called Candles of Joys and Concerns. Congregants would go to the front, light a candle, and say their daughter had been admitted to grad school or their father was in the hospital. Penny and I decided that I should use that time for my announcement.

We were a small congregation and could manage only a half-time minister; Penny came just twice a month. She had been so helpful to me that I wanted to come out on a week she was there. I wasn't ready in March. The next opportunity would be Easter, April 12. After that, Penny was having a shoulder replaced and would be away for two months. That seemed like a long time to wait for my big announcement, so it would have to be Easter.

It was time to let more of the people I cared for in on my secret. I was still presenting myself as the man they had known, although clean-shaven now. I felt I needed to give them the courtesy of knowing what I intended. I had been tempted to just show up in a skirt one Sunday, but I thought it would be better to warn them ahead of time. And, if all went well, I would further build my support network.

I worked on what I would say. I wanted to be clear, and I wanted to let people know how much I appreciated this opportunity. This was a good thing I was doing. I wrote it up and carried the paper with me. Penny asked if I wanted her to read it for me. I said no, but I'd hand her the paper if I faltered.

I had asked Catie to sit with me during the service and asked Ralph to sit in the back – he usually did anyway – and signal me if I wasn't speaking loudly enough. I wanted to go through this only once. I practiced over and over so I could speak what I'd written while looking at the people and not at the paper.

When I arrived at the church Sunday morning, ready and determined, I saw that a number of visitors had shown up. I started having doubts that I'd be able to do it. I wouldn't be speaking only to people I knew. But Penny would be gone for two months. I knew it had to be that day. I went into an empty room and went through some qigong exercises to calm myself.

I sat toward the front, next to Catie. Barbara, an older woman I was friendly with sat next to me. I had talked to Catie about what I was doing but had not come out to Barbara. Yet.

At the appropriate time, I walked to the front of the church, lit a candle with a shaking hand, turned toward the congregation, saw Ralph and Jim at the back, both with big grins, and spoke in a clear voice:

"I light a candle this morning in joy, for this fellowship and for all of you, who have provided a sanctuary here, where I finally feel safe enough to pursue a lifelong dream. In this season of rebirth, I have begun to be reborn ... as a woman, which is what I've *always* wanted to be. I don't know how successful I will be, but already, early in my journey, I have received more understanding and support here than I ever thought possible. It gives me great hope. And I thank you for that."

I walked back to my seat and sat down. Catie squeezed my left hand; Barbara squeezed my right, and the service progressed. I was at peace. I had opened another window and let in more light.

After the service, I went up to the front to gather the collection for deposit, as I always did. A swarm of women gathered around me, happily congratulating me. I don't remember who was there or what they said, other than that one of them gushed, "Now you'll have to find your style!" At the time, I thought that was a really odd comment, but in the months ahead I realized just what she meant.

The social hour after the service was almost overwhelming. I was hugged and congratulated by people I knew well and people I barely knew. A woman told me she had a client who had transitioned successfully at my age. When I told Jim I had been concerned about the visitors' reactions, he said that if they didn't like it then we wouldn't want them anyway, and, "Maybe you should make the announcement every week." My lifelong fears of rejection were fading fast.

A few days later, Sue invited me to her house for tea and scones. Sue was in her eighties and the matriarch of the church. She had been the main one to include me into the church when I'd first arrived. In addition to the church, she was very involved in a number of causes in town. She had pressed me to contribute to some of those causes in the past. She was a small, kindly, well-spoken woman with an iron backbone. She was an effective fundraiser.

At the appointed time, I went to her house with my check-book in my pocket. I was her only guest. She had made the scones herself, and we talked about that in her kitchen while she made the tea. I helped her carry it all into the living room, where we settled on the couch. She poured tea while I helped myself to a scone. I was relaxed, waiting to find out what good cause she was advocating for this time. We settled in with our tea and scones. Then she turned to me and said, in her kind, business-like, little-old-lady voice, "Now, how can the women of the church help you?" I almost fell off the couch. Probably the only thing that kept me from bursting into tears was my utter surprise.

I didn't know what to say to Sue. I stammered, "Just tell me when I'm screwing up." I was venturing into territory I'd only observed. Living in it would be a difficult, complex, wonderful, joyful experience – one that could be filled with pitfalls I, as an outsider, didn't understand. The women of the church became my mentors. I didn't want them to be reluctant to offer advice or criticism. As it turned out, they offered only encouragement, some gentle guidance, and a little good-natured teasing. I was in an odd position – a young girl who was decades older than some of them. To a woman, they handled it well.

One of the women at the church was Lisa – a woman of about 50 who lived alone in a largish house a couple of blocks down the street from me. After my announcement at church, she invited me to go with her and her family to Drag Queen Bingo. Even though this was an annual AIDS fundraiser in Laramie and I'd lived in town for eight years, I'd never heard of it. The organizers of the event brought drag queens from Denver for an evening of food and frivolity. University students attended; local politicians attended; business owners attended. Lisa's daughter was a university student and in the organizing group. She had gotten Lisa and Lisa's parents to agree to attend.

I'm not sure why Lisa asked me to go with her. Possibly she was making the common conflation of all things not hetero-normative – drag queens, transsexuals, transvestites, and maybe gays and lesbians and the genderqueer, too. Or she could have just seen it as what it seemed to me – a fun evening where I could dress however I wanted. At this point I wanted to accept any offer that included me, so I thanked her and said yes.

On the appointed night, I dressed carefully. This would be my first time out in Laramie. New to makeup, I did a poor job. No – make that an awful job. I couldn't see that I was getting any on me, so I kept adding more. It was only at the end of the evening that I realized I looked like I was made up like a kabuki performer. But Lisa and her parents didn't even blink. I hadn't met her parents before, or her daughter, but it was a pleasant evening.

Being Laramie, I of course saw and was recognized by people I knew. The only ones I remember now are the police chief and Lori, the owner of the yarn store. She and Bruce were friends, and I had gotten to know her a bit through him. During Drag Queen Bingo I ran into Lori in the hallway. She gave a start when she saw me but recovered.

A few weeks later, after I'd started living full-time as Katherine, I stopped in to see Lori at her store. She blurted out, "Oh! You don't look nearly as bad as I thought you would," then put her hands over her mouth. "I mean ...." I just laughed and said it was OK, I knew what she meant.

When I was young, I learned to not want what I couldn't have. I wanted a Corvette but knew I would never have one. I wanted to be a girl but saw no way of that happening. It was better not to care. Gretchen's mother would offer me a choice – two different kinds of cookies, perhaps – and I would say that I didn't care. She would reply, "Those that don't care don't get," forcing me to choose. But otherwise I wouldn't choose. I made a lot of decisions by not choosing, letting whatever happened happen. It took a long time for me to get out of that habit.

When I started working on being more open about my gender issues, I didn't dare hope for much. But as each door opened and each threshold was crossed, I wanted to open the next door.

Soon after coming out at church, I was by my garage when my neighbor Steve walked by. He lived two doors down with his wife and their two children of about eight and ten. He was a tall, sturdy man used to hard work, part of a Wyoming ranching and farming family. He taught at the university – something to do with agriculture, I think. He'd always been very friendly and had helped me a number of times with which plants would grow in the harsh Laramie climate. I had started hormones a couple of weeks before but otherwise was as I had been, still dressed as the supposed man he knew. I had not come out to him.

He said "Hi" as he strode by, hurrying to the university campus. But then he stopped and came back. He looked at me more closely and said, "You're going through the change."

I replied, laughing, "Yes Steve, lots of things are changing." He said: "No. You're going through *the* change, aren't you?" A little unsure of where he was going with this, I maintained my smile and said, "Yes, I am." "I've had students who were going through the change. Are you happy?" "Unbelievably happy, Steve."

"Good," he said and walked off toward the university. I don't know how he could tell I was changing, going through the change so early in the process, but he had no problem with it. I went into the house and hugged myself and cried.

But I continued to waver. This was a huge step I was considering. I was standing at the edge, afraid to step off. I had built a successful life as an ersatz man. After 65 years living as a man, could I build a life as a woman? I knew there were people who thought someone like me didn't deserve to live, but I'd managed to build a good support network and was blessed with their encouragement. Perhaps it was time to just risk everything, roll the dice, and deal with the consequences. It wasn't life or death; it was life or not-life.

Two days later, I knew I was ready. Enough wavering – now was the time. I had thought I wouldn't go full-time – live full time as a woman – until the summer. But somehow, I was ready to make the change in late April. I had told everyone I wanted to. I had made several excursions as a woman – to Cheyenne, Denver, Fort Collins, and even Drag Queen Bingo in Laramie. I had started hormones and the long process of removing my facial hair. I was ready.

I dressed in Katherine clothes in the morning, as I usually did. And I began gathering my male clothes. I kept a few items for sentimental reasons, but pretty much everything was leaving the house. I put anything usable into grocery bags to go to the thrift store. The rest went into the trash. I was pretty thorough. There would be no turning back. It felt good to finally close the door on that part of my life – 65 years, 8 months, and 28 days of living as someone I was not. I was ready to start a new life, come what may.

During this time I ate almost every lunch out, rotating among three places in town. Because I went to the same three places so often, most of the front-of-the-house staff knew me. This day I went to the Mexican restaurant because I liked it and because I worried that if I didn't go that day I might never go there again. If I was going to present myself to the world as Katherine, I needed to jump in with both feet.

I presented myself to the hostess. She showed no sign of surprise. She called me señor as she always did and showed me to a seat. The girl who brought the chips looked at me out of the corner of her eyes and called me amigo as she usually did. I realized it would take more than changing my clothes for me to be called señora or amiga. It was hard because I was exposing myself to strangers who knew me, but it was easy because I was in familiar surroundings.

(It was a month or more before I saw Ruben, a waiter I had gotten to know a little. He had been born in Mexico but in high school had moved to L.A. to play football. He spoke English, but it was evident that wasn't his primary language. He'd always been kind, and I enjoyed our brief chats. When I finally saw him, he came to me and said, "I saw a woman sitting here, but then I saw it was you. I'm confused." I explained that I was a woman now and that I'd always wanted to be one. He asked, "Are you happy?" "Yes, wonderfully happy." "Good," he said, "We should all be happy." Yes, Ruben, we should all be happy.)

After my first day living publicly as Katherine, I took a picture of myself. I wanted to document my first day, but when I saw the picture I was horrified. I have always been good at seeing what I want to in the mirror, but I see something else in photos. I was discouraged but wasn't about to turn back.

At my next laser appointment I asked Jody, if she thought I'd make it – be successful in my transition. I reasoned that she'd seen a lot of male-to-female transsexuals, so she'd have some basis for making a judgment. She assured me I'd be OK. "What was it about the picture that made you doubt?" I couldn't think of anything specific, but my chin was not smooth, so I said, "My chin." She gave a little laugh and said, "All women your age have chins like that." My age?

If I was going to live as a woman, I needed to change my name legally. The procedure to change one's name in Wyoming was to file a request with the county court and advertise it in the local paper once a week for four weeks. If no one objected to the court, a judge would grant the request. I called Laurie, the lawyer I knew from church, and asked her to start the process. She explained that the public notices were mainly so people wouldn't avoid their obligations by changing their names. She didn't see why there should be a problem. When the first notice appeared in the paper, I cut it out and pinned it to the church bulletin board.

I didn't read the public notices, but sure enough some people do. My Laramie house was my first with in-ground sprinklers. When I bought the house there was a sticker on the controller for the man who'd installed it. At first I tried caring for the system myself but soon found I didn't have the skills. It was much easier and more effective to call Lou. He was a weathered, semi-retired rancher. He was old Laramie, and I'm sure he pegged me as the city kid I was. After the notice appeared in the newspaper, he came over to do something with the system. Without a hint of judgment in his tone or demeanor, he said he'd seen my name-change request in the paper. I said yes, I was changing my name to Katherine. He looked at me, giving nothing away, nodded, and that was that.

While I waited for the new legal name, I told more and more people I was now Katherine. Most everyone was good about calling me Katherine, or Kate. I couldn't change my name at the official places until the court acted, but I could write to or tell all of my friends, everyone on my Christmas list, the many people who knew me by first name but didn't necessarily know my last name, and, it seemed, many, many more. I was just so happy to be Katherine that I wanted to tell everyone – even people I didn't know.

I thought I might manage to be Katherine but could only aspire to being Kate. In my mind, Katherine was more reserved than Kate – Katherine might be smarter but Kate was more fun. My friends gradually began shortening Katherine to Kate. I corrected the one man who tried to shorten it to Kathy. And corrected him again until he stopped it.

The turning point for me was when I told one of my favorite baristas. She was a perky ranch girl studying at the university. When I asked her name, she had said, "Morgan ... like the horse," and whinnied. When I told her I was now Katherine, she grinned, stuck out her hand, and said, "Hi Kate." I decided I could be Kate after all.

And one more thing about Kate: When I chose the name Katherine, I had forgotten that my great-grandmother Birdsall was Kate, not Katherine – Kate Birdsall. I never knew her – she died about five years before I was born – but I find it nice to have that connection to her.

I usually don't remember my dreams, but about this time I had one I can remember still.

~

I am in my car following a sort-of friend as she drives to a party. She's driving faster than I want. I'd had a few drinks earlier and, while I was OK to drive, I wasn't as competent as I wanted to be, going at that speed on that road that was edged with sand as it curved, I was having a hard time keeping up.

The road passes through part of a military base. Usually you just drive through, but they lower a gate and stop my friend. I slow down and wonder whether I should turn around, but they lower another gate behind me to stop me. I realize then that I've forgotten my purse and have no ID.

They take me to a place that is part hospital and part detention center. It is a little chaotic there. It has people with injuries and people they want to interrogate and people they are just detaining. I am in a hospital gown with a light robe, sitting in a chair like a hairdresser's chair. They are examining me – nothing intrusive, just asking questions and looking in my mouth. I don't know if I will be in trouble for driving without a license or driving while not completely sober. I don't know if I will be allowed to go back home to get my purse.

One rather abrupt doctor thunks my stomach and walks off, returning with a box about the size of a Kleenex box. In it are pills to settle my stomach – antacids or something. I munch on one and begin to feel better. I notice that there are other things in the box – a comb and some other things – like a small CARE package.

One of the other patients tries to grab my box of stuff. I hug it to me and ask the doctor if I can keep it. He assures me that it is mine to keep.

Then I start crying, holding the box against me. I have no purse and no identity and they have given me a little package of stuff to help me be all right. The doctor asks why I am crying.

I say: "You've been so kind to me and you don't even know who I am." He says: "We know who you are, Katherine."

He didn't say my old name when he said "We know who you are." He said "We know who you are, Katherine."

I hug the box closer and wake up crying, tears running down my cheeks.

∿

I was beginning to believe dreams have meaning.

I gained confidence as I continued my life in Laramie without incident. I did pretty much what I had been doing but now as Katherine. I took care of my house and yard, ate in town almost every lunch, shopped at the same stores, talked to the same people, and continued to serve on the church board. I went to the same doctor and dentist and ophthalmologist. I had the same insurance agent, the same neighbors, the same friends, plus some new ones. My life was the same as it had been, but everything was different.

Laramie is a town of some notoriety for the brutal killing of Matt Shepard, a gay university student, in 1998. The ease with which most people accepted my change was rather amazing, especially given this history. It is a small town, and many people knew me or at least were familiar with me. Six months earlier I had presented myself as a bearded man. Now I presented myself as a woman. The change probably seemed sudden to them – I'm surprised they didn't suffer whiplash.

During one of my counseling sessions about this time, I was happily bubbling away to Judith about what I was doing and the reactions of the people I met. Usually she was serious and careful in what she said to me, but this day she started laughing, saying, "You have always been so cautious and concerned with not making waves or causing discomfort, but with this it is more, 'Here I am, ready or not!'"

Marian told me, "This is going very fast and everyone is having trouble keeping up." I still had doubts now and then, but I really wanted to continue. I was riding this wave of emotion, of liberation, of hope, and I didn't want to get off. The process had taken on a life of its own, and I didn't know if I could stop it or slow it down even if I wanted to. A friend told me what I was doing was a big change. But somehow I saw it more as growth or evolution than change. To me it was a blossoming.

I got a lot of support and encouragement, but not everyone was happy. My next-door neighbor, a Spanish-American man whose family had lived in Colorado when it belonged to Mexico, had always been very friendly and helpful. We had talks over the back fence about the neighborhood and loaned each other tools. But when I started dressing exclusively in women's clothes, he had trouble acknowledging me. He told me that his church – a non-denominational Evangelical Christian church on the edge of town – told him I was born this way. I don't remember his exact words, but I had the impression he was conflating transgender with gay. However, he had trouble accepting my change and ignored me as best he could. His wife, on the other hand, was perhaps even more friendly than she had been.

At lunch one day, I was sitting at my favorite table at one of my regular restaurants, talking to one of the servers. I had been showing up as Kate for a few weeks by then. He told me about a married couple, a man and a woman, who came in most Sundays, both dressed as women. He offered to connect me with them if I wanted. I told him, "No, this is permanent for me." He replied, looking directly at my chest, "So those are real?" I had to laugh. "Not yet, Ben, but I'll let you know when they are."

I loved my life. I was comfortable with who I was. After a life-time of quiet demeanor, I became chatty. I would look people in the eyes, smile more, engage them in conversation. After living so many years holding myself in, suddenly my hands waved around when I talked, of their own volition. I had always held myself back, but now I found myself touching others – a hand or sleeve or shoulder. I had been closed; now I was open. And I smiled. A lot.

Living full time as a woman was a dream come true despite how uncertain and afraid I'd been. But there were two effects I hadn't thought through completely. One was the practical matter of clothes. I had my crossdressing clothes, but many of them had been bought because they were cheap or because they fulfilled some fantasy and were not intended to be worn outside my house. I loved my crinoline, but it wasn't practical for street wear in Laramie, Wyoming. I figured I had a tough enough road to walk without looking weird or outlandish. I came to think of it as being a bit like your house burning down and getting amnesia at the same time – you've lost all of your clothes and don't know what works for you. I had yet to find my style.

The other effect was that at times I felt almost like I had two people going on in me at the same time – a lifelong demeanor of being "he" with the memories and habits of being him, and the new demeanor of "she." I was still one person and was still very much the same person, but I was trying to become Kate and discover who she would be. I wasn't just playing a role, pretending to be her. I was becoming her at the same time I had always been her. To some extent, I had to suppress him and perhaps even deny him as me just to give her room to grow. It could get confusing. And I was living it. How confusing was it for others, with no skin in the game, with little incentive?

I didn't know whether I wanted genital surgery. I didn't know whether I needed it. I had changed to being socially female, and that was the main thing I wanted – to be seen as, and to be treated as, a woman.

I knew I didn't want facial contouring. I was fortunate that I didn't have a lot of male skull development – the heavy jaw, the large brow ridge, and the other large features we identify as male. I had some, but I looked male, not masculine. Plus, I was 65 years old. No amount of surgery would change that.

I didn't want breast implants. I would develop breasts to some extent just on the hormones. And there was always padding. When my sister asked about it, I told her the conventional wisdom was that I'd get one cup smaller than my sister. She replied, "Then you wouldn't have anything!"

But I'd come this far. Each step was better, and now the next step was genital surgery – what used to be called a sex change but by then was called gender or sex reassignment surgery (GRS or SRS). As of this writing, I think it is called gender confirmation surgery. Regardless of what it is called, the surgery removes the testicles and reshapes the rest to form a vagina. Well, I thought, why not?

At one session of the Fort Collins support group, people talked about getting surgery in Trinidad. To their amusement, I said something about not wanting to go to a Caribbean island for surgery. Laughing, they said they meant Trinidad, Colorado. Feeling clueless – a very familiar feeling for me – I learned that a gynecologist who performed this specialized surgery was an easy five hour drive from my house. In fact, the first such operation in the US was done there in 1969 by the doctor who had trained the current one. For years "a trip to Trinidad" had been code for getting what in the 70s was called a sex-change operation.

I looked on the surgeon's website and read about the physical requirements – primarily to be of reasonably good health. They advised against smoking and some other activities that would make it more difficult to recover. The surgery was extensive and they wanted the body to be strong enough to withstand the assault. Concerned I might be too old, I called the office. "Oh no," the nurse said, "Our oldest patient was 82." I thought, "God bless her, to finally get what she needed after all those years."

The surgeon's waiting list was ten months long. I would be required to live full time as a woman for a year before I could have the surgery. That seemed plenty long enough for me to change my mind, but I needed to get on the list. I sent the paperwork and my deposit, feeling more and more that this was the right path for me.

One question to resolve before the surgery was whether I wanted a neo-vagina or what they called cosmetic surgery, where the external look was the same but there was no actual vagina. It was either/or. Once cosmetic surgery was done, it would be exceedingly difficult to form a vagina later – the extra tissue needed for it would have been discarded during the first surgery.

I talked to my friend Sarah about it. She was about my age and had not, as far as I knew, had a male partner in more than 20 years. I told her the cosmetic surgery sounded easier, and that I'd probably never have penetrative sex anyway. She replied, with a little grin, "You never know." I applied for the full surgery.

I had never been interested in being with a man. I'd gotten some offers through the years, but I just wasn't interested. However, when the testosterone was blocked and I was taking estrogen, there were times when I would see a man and have a funny feeling in the pit of my stomach. Conventional wisdom was that one-third of transsexuals would retain the same attraction, one-third would switch, and one-third would become asexual. I've never seen anything about this other than rumor, but I thought that if it was true perhaps I was now attracted to men rather than women, or perhaps both. Even if I did become attracted to men, I didn't think any man would ever be attracted to me. But there was Sarah and her "You never know."

One of my fears was how police would react to me being male but presenting female. Having associated with gay men for much of my life, I'd heard lots of stories. There was the history of police raids on gay bars and the unpleasantness that ensues. It wasn't just the Stonewall raid and subsequent protests. It was a long history of the police trying to enforce social norms that penalized and sometimes brutalized those of us who fall outside those norms. I'd had no bad experiences with law enforcement, but living as female even though physically male moved me outside my previous middle-class white comfort zone. I knew that many officers are sensitive to the many nuances of human behavior, but I also knew that the field can attract those who want opportunities to impose their will on others.

The university campus sat between my house and the church, with 15th Street the only city street to cut through the campus. I went back and forth to the church several times a week, to meetings and chores and Sunday services. Fifteenth was my regular route. Because the street cuts across campus, the city decided to lower the speed limit through that section.

Soon after the speed limit changed, I buzzed along 15th on my way to church one morning, thinking about setting it up for Sunday service. Then there were flashing lights behind me. I had started living full time but my name change hadn't come through, so my license still had my old name and picture, but I was dressed in blouse, skirt, hose, and heels. I pulled onto a side street and stopped.

When the officer came up to my car, I said, berating myself, "I know, I know. They just lowered the speed limit and you always patrol more heavily after a change. I just wasn't thinking," and handed him my license.

He went back to his car to look for priors on this crazy person. He came back, handed me my license, and told me to slow down next time. And so once again my fears were not realized. And yes, I was much more careful driving across the campus after that.

12

DECLARING ✳ 2009

"You'll never know who you are unless you shed who you pretend to be."

— Vironika Tugaleva

Four weeks after I had applied to change my name, my attorney, Laurie, called me on a Friday afternoon to say my name change was complete. I raced over to the courthouse before it closed for the weekend, and took the papers to Staples to have a dozen copies made. It was too late to do anything more with the papers that day, and Monday was a holiday – Memorial Day – so I'd have to wait through the weekend. And it's just as well. I was unbelievably excited. It was one thing to say I was Katherine; it was another for the Wyoming District Court to say I was. It was just so very, very validating.

I made an appointment with Susan to do my hair first thing Tuesday morning. I wanted to look my best for my driver's license picture. I went to church on Sunday, as I almost always did. And I spent the Monday holiday picking up trash along my section of

Adopt-a-Highway, a distracting and quieting task alone on a two-lane road out on the open prairie.

I had calmed down by Tuesday morning, but this was going to be a big day. After getting my hair done, I drove to the DMV office on the south edge of town. It was staffed by two middle-aged women who had worked there for a long time. They couldn't have been nicer when I showed up with my court order.

I filled out the paperwork and handed it in. One of the women took my picture, showed it to me, and asked if I wanted her to retake it, but I was happy enough with her first try. She finished up, gave me a temporary license with my new name on it, told me the permanent one would come in the mail in four to six weeks, and wished me well. I was official.

With my new license and the pack of name-change copies, I drove the 50 miles to the Air Force base in Cheyenne. I went to the back gate because I knew the ID card office was in that part of the base. A young airman was staffing the gate. I handed him my ID card as I usually did, not thinking much about it. He looked at the card, at me, and at the card again. He said, "Uh, Mrs. Birdsall...?" I finally realized what was happening and said, with a smile, "Oh yeah. I've changed my name and need to get a new ID card."

The wheels in his head turned and he realized there'd been a few other changes, too. He bent down to the window and gestured: "Go down this road, turn left at the second light. It'll be the first building on your right, ma'am." He handed me my card and saluted. Bless the younger generation.

The ID card office was in a large building with other offices and who knows what else. The building was under lockdown when I got there. Rather than wait in the cold wind of the parking lot, I went to the Base Exchange to use the restroom. There, when I came out of the stall, a woman who washing her hands started chatting away happily to me about the weather that day.

The social conventions of men's and women's restrooms are

very different. On the internet forum, there are any number of threads about those differences. Some threads mention that in a women's room one might encounter a Chatty Woman – a person whose behavior is unknown in men's rooms. I encountered my first Chatty Woman on F. E. Warren Air Force Base on the day I was changing my name. Since then I've encountered any number of others and have enjoyed them all.

When I got back to the ID card office, I could get into the building. I signed in and waited my turn, listening to the thirty-something civilian woman in charge dressing down the young airman working for her for not showing up for work when he should have. I was becoming concerned that they'd both be in a bad mood when it was my turn.

Fortunately, I was called by the woman rather than the now-surly airman. She was very professional at first, but as we talked she relaxed and we grew comfortable with each other while she processed my paperwork. She said she'd take care of DEERS (the Defense Enrollment Eligibility Reporting System) and Tricare (my health insurance). I told her I was still legally male but didn't see any gender marker on the ID card, unless it was in the codes on the back. She assured me there was no gender marker and, as a retiree, the card would be good for the rest of my life. She wished me well.

On a roll and already in Cheyenne, I headed to the Social Security office. There, I got a number and sat waiting while a succession of people went to the window and made excuses for not doing what they were supposed to do. Surely this woman, I thought, would be grumpy when it was my turn. But she wasn't. Perhaps she was relieved I was a simple name-change rather than yet another problem. We chatted easily as she completed the paperwork. She assured me I didn't have to do anything additional to change my name with Medicare.

I went to lunch and then headed back to Laramie. I raced

around town, dropping name-change copies at the pharmacy, dentist, doctors, counselor, insurance office, cable office, credit union, and bank. Everyone was very nice about it. The next day I changed the titles for the car and my two motorcycles.

When I went to the county offices to change the name on my voter registration, the woman there was nice, and I was comfortable with her. Then she asked my gender. "I didn't know it made any difference for voting," I said. She replied, "It's just for our records." "Gee, I don't know. I'm still legally male and Wyoming won't let me change it until I have surgery." We talked a bit more about it. Finally she said, patting me on the forearm, "Why don't I just leave it blank. You can let us know when you get it all straightened out."

I had seen the name change as just one more step in the process, but it was a much bigger deal to me than I had supposed it would be. It was saying: "I am no longer that person. I am this person now." In a way, it was "I am this person now, like it or not." Even more than the clothes, I was declaring myself. I had shut the door on him; now I was her.

The thing with transitioning is that it is a selfish act. I was becoming Kate – or declaring to the world that I am really Kate after all – and expecting the rest of the world to change their habits, use my new name and refer to me as she or her. People were really good about it. There were a few slip-ups with the name, but usually the person caught themselves right away. The pronouns were more difficult. It hurt to hear a "he," especially if the speaker didn't catch it. I would correct them most times, but I understood that it wasn't intentional. I was aware that I was asking others to wrap their heads around something I barely understood myself. And I was asking them to do it not for them but for me.

The Saturday after my name-change I drove down to Colorado to stay with my sister, Marty and her husband, Joe. Their 50th wedding anniversary was coming up in June. When I started moving toward living as Kate, I had expected to wait until after their anniversary to go full-time. But I hadn't waited. Now we needed to figure out how to handle this.

Joe had been supportive from the start, but Marty had mourned the loss of her little brother for a month or two. She was supportive but didn't understand it. Or not supportive, exactly, not in an active way. More accepting, I guess, in part because I was going to do it regardless, and she wanted to keep the connection with me.

I had told her that I would leave it to her about the anniversary – I could come as my old self, as Kate (my new self), or not at all: her choice. I spent the weekend so she could see the new me.

We talked most of the afternoon. Standing in the backyard, she criticized me for male behavior when I bent, without thinking, to pick up her dropped tissue. I saw it as the more nimble of us helping the one with mobility limitations, but I had done it automatically, without thinking, and I could see Marty's point. At the end of the afternoon, she asked me to come to the anniversary party as her brother.

We spent the evening together and went to our beds. When I stayed with them, I always got up first, then Joe, and some hours later, Marty. Joe would prepare the coffee pot before he went to bed so that I could just start it in the morning and drink coffee while waiting for him to get up.

By the time Joe got up, I was almost in tears. I told him of Marty's decision to have me attend as her brother, but I just couldn't do it. He seemed to understand and said I needed to tell her. When she got up, I again explained that I had waited too long for this and had wanted it too much. I was very sorry but I couldn't come as her brother – it would just be too hard. I couldn't go back, even for a few hours, even for her. I'm not sure that she understood, but she said I could come as Kate.

I obviously didn't understand when I thought I could switch

back and forth. There was the old, hiding me and the new, open me. But there was only one me. I found that somehow we expand once we let ourselves out of our cages, and that it's really hard to cram us back inside.

When the day of the party came a month later, I drove down to their house early enough to get there before the guests. The party was to be an informal affair in the backyard with relatives, friends, and neighbors. I came into the house to find a receiving line of family – my nephew and his wife, her parents, Joe's niece and her husband and their two teen-age daughters, Joe's nephew, Joe's sister and her husband, and I don't remember who else. Other than Marty and Joe, none of them had seen me since I'd become Kate. Each person in the line shook my hand in welcome, calling me Kate or Aunt Kate.

And the party began. I spent the afternoon talking to friends and relatives of Marty and Joe, some of whom I'd known for a long time and some I hadn't met until that day. It was a wonderful party – formal enough to be an event but informal enough to be relaxed.

When it was time for me to leave, I said good-bye to Marty and went to find Joe. He was in the backyard talking to someone I didn't know and Larry, the son of his longtime friend and co-worker. I'd known Larry, peripherally, all of his life.

When I came up to the group to say good-bye to Joe, Larry came up to me, grinning, standing too close, and said, "Have we met before?" I replied, smiling, "Well, actually, we have." Still standing too close, he said something about not remembering me. I replied, with downcast eyes, "Well, she probably wouldn't want me to tell you, but I used to be Marty's brother." I said good-bye to Joe and left.

It was only in the car, driving away, that it struck me: He was hitting on me, the jerk. The incident said more about Larry than it did about any attractiveness of mine, but I was pleased, in an odd way.

Joe later told me that Larry's teenage son had told Marty, in a mix of outrage and disgust, that I was "a man." She had taken him aside, trying to help him understand. I was sorry to detract from her big day, but for the most part the afternoon was a wonderful celebration.

Later that June, my friend Bren and I went together to Salt Lake City for General Assembly (GA) – the annual convention for Unitarian Universalists. She wouldn't have been able to go if she didn't share the hotel room, and sharing the room would have been awkward if I hadn't started living as Kate.

The 400-mile drive from Laramie was easy. She and I were comfortable together, talking or not, across the wide-open spaces of southern Wyoming, stopping for coffee and again for lunch.

This was the first GA for either of us. About 4,000 UUs had gathered at the convention center. It was exciting as we were swept up into the activities. I know that I was identifiable as transgender to some people, but I had no way to know how many. I was just me, one of the delegates to the convention.

The main women's restroom was a hive of activity and talk. It was large, with perhaps 50 stalls. At times the noise level would get really high, as women greeted each other and happily chatted, bustling between the sinks and hand dryers, some running into old friends or coordinating a later meeting. It was a happy place, and I loved it. I don't know what the similar-sized men's room was like, but I'd been in enough men's rooms through the years to think it was probably far less joyful.

Bren and I went to different workshops but would meet for lunch and business meetings. We had a good time but became exhausted as the week wore on. One afternoon we skipped out and walked to Temple Square. Touring the museum, I was surprised when an older, well-dressed guide seemed to be hitting on me. Like Larry, he probably didn't even know that was how he came across. The window to Woman World inched wider.

But it was uneven. One evening at a restaurant in Salt Lake City with Bren and a couple of others, I went to the women's restroom. There were two women at the sink, talking to each other. As I closed myself in the stall, I heard the room door open as they left and one of the women whisper to the other, "That's a man!"

A childhood friend of mine was also at GA. We had reconnected the previous year after five decades of no contact. Jan lived in Las Cruces, New Mexico now, and she was in a long-term relationship with another woman. Jan wore flannel shirts, no makeup, and cropped hair. She was busy working GA, so we didn't spend much time together, but we sat together for the Sunday service. Being Sunday, I'd dressed in skirt and heels. At one point in the service, she elbowed me in the ribs and said, "You'll never make it as a lesbian, Kate. You look too good." I smiled and said, "That's not what I'm trying to do here, Jan."

At one point during that Sunday service, we were standing, listening to the minister give an invocation. I don't remember exactly what he said, but I had to sit down as my eyes filled with tears. After so many years feeling like I was on the outside, hearing sincere words of inclusion moved me deeply.

13

VENTURING ✳ 2009-2010

"there are journeys from which one cannot return"
— Cristina Peri Rossi, *The Ship of Fools*

I didn't come out to my neighbors, but of course they had noticed the change. I knew everyone on my block and half the people on the next one. My neighbor next door was trying to ignore me, but my good relationship with Steve and his family in the next house continued. In the house next to Steve was Bob and his wife and their two children of about eight and twelve.

In Laramie, we didn't see our neighbors very much in the long winters, but one afternoon during the summer I was walking past Bob's house on my way home from the park. Bob was in his front yard. I had been living as Katherine for about three months by then.

We greeted each other as we usually did. Then he said: "I just wanted to tell you that you are doing a wonderful thing for the neighborhood." Puzzled but smiling, I replied, "Gee, Bob, I'm really doing it for myself." "Yeah, but my kids are asking the *best* questions." Laughing, I told him, "Glad I could help," and waved good-bye. If I was going to walk off the cliff, it was a nice neighborhood to do it in.

(The only other neighbors to ever say anything to me lived across the street. They were a couple in their mid-fifties. I had gotten to know them a little, sometimes sipping wine with them in their back yard during long summer evenings. They were intrigued by my transition, particularly after my surgery. Sitting together one evening, Dean offered to try out my new vagina for me. I declined politely, saying that I would wait for someone who wasn't married.)

Going to the conference in Salt Lake City had built my confidence. I had been accepted as Kate, even by those who recognized that I had lived as a man. Settling in back home, I was gratified by the reactions of the people of Laramie. I had been afraid of coming out, showing the part of me I'd kept hidden all those years. I was mostly afraid of rejection, being mocked, ostracized, thought ridiculous. But I was also very aware of the possibility of physical violence. The Laramie I knew was very inclusive, but there were elements in the area that were not. And it was Wyoming. I feared reaction from people I thought of as The Enforcers – individuals with narrow views of how things should be and who feel entitled to enforce those views. I thought it entirely possible that my house could be sprayed with bullets some night.

I asked an acquaintance about what I could do. He was a big man, an avid hunter and fisherman, and led the local Harley club – a man of more conservative views than mine. When I visited him after starting to live as Katherine, sitting in his living room that was made smaller by all the heads of dead animals crowding out from the walls, he told me, "I just have to tell you, it takes a lot of *balls* to do what you're doing." I laughed and said, "Well, Pete, actually that's the problem. But thank you." After all, I knew what he meant.

On his advice I put a "retired Coast Guard" license plate frame on my car and a sticker on the door. I also bought a short-barreled shotgun that I kept, loaded, under my bed.

And I signed up for a concealed carry course at the shooting range outside town. I'd had weapons training in the Army and Coast Guard, but it'd been years since I handled a gun. I was a pretty good shot, sometimes. The Army Colt .45 handgun was too heavy for me, and I had trouble hitting anything more than about ten feet away. The Coast Guard .38 was much more manageable – with it I could hit a target at over 25 feet. I thought that if I was going to have a gun in the house, a safety refresher was a really good idea.

There were about ten of us in the class. A 20-something and I were the only women. Only some of the men were hunters, but they all were confident they already knew everything about guns. The instructor was a smallish man about my age who looked like he'd been left out in the weather too long. He was one of these guys who wouldn't walk out to the mailbox by the road without a handgun strapped on.

For some reason, he took a shine to me. With his attention, I regained my skills and then some. I would go out to the range between classes to practice. Sometimes he'd wander over from his makeshift house next to the range. One day, when I caught him looking at me with googly eyes, I had an unprecedented reaction. I began imagining living out there with him and cooking for him. What the *hell* was going on?! I didn't even cook for myself, not even considering that he was totally inappropriate for me. *Damn* these hormones! After that I wore my wedding ring when I went out to the range.

The day I went to the sheriff's office to apply for my concealed carry permit, I was feeling really perky. I had dressed in a pencil skirt and medium heels and had eaten a relaxed lunch in town. I was feeling good so decided to apply for the permit that day.

The woman deputy behind the counter in the sheriff's office was professional in her uniform, but we had an ease of familiarity with each other that made me think I might have met her somewhere else. I filled out the form and explained that I had checked "male" on the application because I was still legally male. I couldn't change my gender marker in Wyoming until I'd had "irreversible surgery."

She thought that would be fine. Then I asked her if I'd have to go through the whole process again once I could change the marker.

"Gee, I don't know," she said. We talked about it a bit, but finally she said she should go check – the detective who handled the permits was in the office. She went into the back office and was gone awhile. I expected her to ask him herself, but when she came back he was behind her. He had on his good detective face, all seriousness, and said, "Yes?"

Evidently she hadn't told him my question. Still feeling chipper, I said, "I'm still legally male. When I'm legally female, will I have to apply for the permit again?"

Nothing.

He stood there blank, expressionless, not moving. It was like time had stopped. I waited a bit and then repeated in the same chirpy voice, "Well, I'm legally male. When I'm finally legally female will I have to apply again?"

After a pause, he relaxed, smiled broadly, and said gently in a sweet voice, "Yes. You'll have to apply again."

He went back to his office. I talked with the deputy a bit more. She gave me paperwork to complete the process. As I headed across the street to get fingerprinted at the jail, I thought I'd never seen anyone's mind so completely blown before. I wondered if the deputy had set him up.

The jail was a scary place. I was buzzed into the windowless building through a heavy metal door. The anteroom was good-sized and seemed to be made of concrete and steel, with several doors made of bars leading off to other parts of the building. I resolved to do what I could to avoid being brought there involuntarily.

I handed my paperwork to the woman deputy. She was professional, neutral but not cold. She looked over the paperwork and asked if this was my maiden name. I said, "Well, I'm transsexual and I've changed my first name but not my last."

Without skipping a beat, she asked "Oh. What was that name?" I realized she just needed the information for the background check and told her. Her attitude didn't change in any way. She fingerprinted me and told me the next steps.

It was quite an experience. The women were unfazed, the man was sweet, and I was reassured.

I was a little concerned about showing my new self to the car mechanics and at the motorcycle shops. These seemed like guy domains, and in my experience guy domains enforce a code of guy-ness that doesn't allow a lot of flexibility. I'd owned a series of Honda cars in the years I lived in Laramie and had gotten friendly with some of the mechanics at the local dealer. We'd joke and talk when I brought in my car. I'd even borrowed a few tools from them on occasion, to work on my trailer.

The first time I brought in my car while dressed in a skirt and calling myself Kate, it seemed to me that nothing changed as far as they were concerned. The only difference I could see was that perhaps they began treating me a little more gently, as they would any woman. I don't mean they discounted me, as some men do to women around machines. They were just a little more kind. From what I could see, their acceptance was seamless. I had respected them as mechanics and as nice guys. Even though I had changed from him to her, they never disappointed me.

I didn't get my motorcycles serviced locally. I'd been taking them to a small independent shop in Fort Collins, which was run by a husband-and-wife team. They had met riding motorcycles and ran the shop as the family business it was – he in the back and she in the front. Because I rode so many miles each year, I had been a frequent customer of theirs and had gotten to know them a little. After I had begun living full time as Kate, I drove my car to Fort Collins for some errands and stopped by the motorcycle shop. When I walked in, they both were at the counter, bent over some paperwork. They recognized me, of course, and looked a little startled. He asked, "Is this permanent?" I assured him it most definitely was. He said, "OK then," and seemed to be satisfied. His wife stuck out her hand with a big grin and said, "Congratulations!" He went back into the service area. With no other customers in the shop, she talked with me for an hour or so about women's riding gear and how to stay safe when riding alone as a woman.

This shop sold used bikes but it wasn't an authorized dealer. When I wanted a new bike, I had gone to the dealer in Aurora, on the south edge of Denver, some 150 miles south of Laramie. This was a very different operation than the little shop in Fort Collins. The Aurora dealer was the largest of its kind between St Louis and California. I didn't go there often, being so far away, but through the years I had become friendly with the manager, a man of about 50 who seemed well suited to running a large, modern, busy motorcycle dealership. The first time I showed up as Kate, we talked in his office for quite some time. He'd had another customer who was transsexual. The manager was disgusted by some of the ignorance this woman had contended with at his shop. He asked me to tell him if any of his staff were at all disrespectful. I wasn't as familiar to them, so I had little to gage any change in their behavior. They always treated me well, in a business-like manner, both before and after my transition to being Kate.

So once again my fears didn't come to anything. I don't think the fears were baseless – I knew of too many incidents, ranging from unpleasantness to murder, on which to base them. It was just that I encountered very little of what I had feared. Those who had gone before me had helped smooth the way.

I continued my weekly trips to Fort Collins for laser treatments. When Jody had done as much as she thought she could, she recommended Angie, an electrologist. Jody and Angie were used to working together, so it was easy to transfer my weekly visits from one to the other. When I started going to Angie, she worked in the back room of a hair salon on the south side of Fort Collins, but sometime later she got her own place a couple of miles closer to the city center. She was fun to spend time with, too, although the treatments were more painful. Because she worked only on my face and had to be precise, placing the needle alongside each hair down to the root, our conversations were more one-sided than when I was with Jody. Angie sent me back to Jody a few times when she would discover an area of dark hairs. A zap of the laser would clear an area about the size of a dime; electrolysis worked hair by hair. Angie was careful, but some areas – particularly the jawline, under the nose, and around the mouth – were very sensitive. My doctor gave me a prescription for a numbing cream. I would put it on when I left Laramie and apply another coat when I got to Angie's. The cream was only marginally helpful.

To make it easier for Angie to see the hairs, I wouldn't shave for a couple of mornings before a treatment. I took my electric razor with me and shaved the areas she hadn't worked on once I left. Gradually over the months, there was less and less to shave. It was a long, tedious process.

There were a few weeks I went twice, but once a week was about all I could take, and Angie said my skin had to recover between treatments. I wanted to go every week, to get it done and over with, but there were a few times in the winter when the roads were either closed or just too difficult because of ice and blowing snow. In 2009 I put over 20,000 miles on the car, while never venturing out of the three-county area of Laramie, Cheyenne, and Fort Collins, except for a couple of visits to my sister, one more county south. Most of the mileage was going for hair-removal treatments and to the support group. I was glad I didn't have a job that required me to show up for forty hours a week. Actually, I did have a job: shedding the male me so that Katherine could finally live in the open air.

In the fall, I asked Angie if she thought we'd be done by the end of the year. She said she thought that it might take a little longer than that, being purposely vague so I wouldn't be discouraged. The average male face has 30,000 hairs, and at best Angie was zapping a few hundred each session. Over time, I went less and less frequently, but in the end it took six years of treatments to get my face to a point where I can pluck the few hairs that show up now and then. But the treatments were worth it. They did a lot to soften my features and help make me more presentable as a woman.

Some male-to-female transsexuals who transition after their twenties contend with thinning hair and have to wear wigs. With a full head of thick hair, I was – again – one of the lucky ones. My hair went a long way toward making me presentable as a woman.

When I was in my thirties, I had asked my barber about all the hair I found in the shower and bathroom sink. He told me not to worry about it until I could see where it came from, so I didn't.

Living as a man, I didn't check my appearance that often. But when I started trying to appear to others as a woman, I looked at myself more closely. I'd always had a high forehead, but one morning, inspecting my hairline, I could see that the edge was weak and receding.

Oh no! My father had a bald spot at his crown; both my father's brother and my brother had thinning hair on top. Any male pattern baldness should have stopped when I switched to female hormones, but I was afraid that perhaps it was progressing anyway. What was I to do?

I made an appointment with a Cheyenne doctor who specialized in treating hair loss. She inspected my hairline closely and talked about some possible treatments. I suggested a treatment I'd read about. She said it wasn't tested for efficacy on women and continued inspecting my scalp. I again suggested this other treatment. She again dismissed it.

I said, "Perhaps there's something you should know..." A month or so earlier I had been told by a cosmetician that I had "male skin." Trusting her assessment, I assumed that anyone trained and experienced at looking closely at skin – hairdressers, cosmeticians, laser and electrolysis technicians, dermatologists, etc. – would know I was transsexual without being told. Besides, I still had to shave my face daily. I had assumed this woman who had been trained to look at hair growing from skin and now, looking closely at mine, would immediately recognize my "male skin," but maybe not.

I told her I was transsexual. She said, "Well, you fooled *me*." She said a few more things about my hair, interspersed with a few more you-fooled-mes. She declared my baldness was just male pattern baldness and left the room, upset that I had fooled her. I felt really bad about it. I said to the nurse, in a meek voice, "I'm not trying to fool anyone. I'm just trying to live my life." She smiled sympathetically and showed me out.

It hurt me to hurt the doctor, for her to think I was trying to trick people. But I was also secretly glad to be so believable as a woman.

Actually, perhaps I was trying to fool people. Not trick them, but perhaps slide through without them noticing. There was no question in Laramie, where I had known way too many people before, but perhaps when I went other places.

I remember reading many years ago that the first thing we

notice about someone is their gender. It's an unconscious reaction and usually happens in a split second. We don't even know we're doing it. But when their gender isn't recognizable immediately, it interrupts that. We might stare, or ponder. That's one reason the older generation will sometimes complain about the younger generation's mode – it interrupts that subconscious process. In my day, it was boys starting to wear longer hair, like the Beatles and others.

For me, living as Kate was much more than wearing a skirt or heels, much more than whatever changes I might make to my body. For me, it was living as a woman – just another woman, immediately and unconsciously recognized as one of the sisterhood of women. That was where I belonged, and that is where I wanted to live.

I'd been doing pretty well, but I continued to worry whether that was possible.

Through the summer and fall I continued on a high. My newfound openness and my new life were intoxicating. In late September we got our first snowstorm of the season. It was like I was five years old again. I raced around the house getting dressed in skirt and boots and drove up to a small road above Laramie. I wanted a picture of me – the new me – in the snow. I set up the tripod and posed for several pictures, but I couldn't relax to smile without grimacing in the cold gale. Undaunted, I drove back home and set up in my backyard. I happily ran back and forth, setting the camera, posing, then checking the result. None of the pictures were very good as photographs, but they do show me just so very, very happy.

Most of my life I had thought I had a very prominent nose. With all these modifications I was doing and planning to do, I thought perhaps a nose job would help my appearance. I asked Kurt, my doctor, for a recommendation. He said he liked the work of a doctor in Fort Collins. I called her office to set up a consult.

When I went to see her, she asked what I had come for. I said, "My nose." When she replied, "Why?" I thought that perhaps I didn't need a nose job. We talked about it a bit. A nose job isn't just a re-contouring, she explained, but was essentially breaking the nose, reshaping it, and letting it heal. Ugh. She took some pictures and showed me how much reshaping was possible that would still let me breathe through my nose easily when done. It wasn't worth it – the change would be minor.

She then started to talk to me about an eye tuck to pull back the skin that was hooding the outer corners of my eyes, and perhaps surgery to tighten my jowls. We talked for a while until I cried, "I'm not that vain!"

She said, "But you're a 66 year-old woman."

Surprising myself, I burst into tears, sobbing out, "I never expected to be either."

When I calmed down, we talked some more. We agreed on the eye tuck. We'd see how that went before considering the jowl tightening. I'd always prided myself in never having had elective surgery – I didn't consider GRS to be elective – but here I was, going to get an eye tuck.

If I could stand for her to do it while awake, she could do it in her office. If I needed a general anesthetic, she'd have to do it at the hospital, doubling the cost. I told her, in almost a little-girl voice, "I was in the Army. I can be tough."

On the appointed day, my friend Sharon drove me through blowing snow on icy roads to Fort Collins. She waited for me for the hour or so it took to get my eyes fixed. The procedure wasn't painful, but it was interesting, and I was glad to be awake to experience it. Then Sharon drove me home. (Thank you Sharon.)

After the operation, I wasn't supposed to lie down for 36 hours. So for two days I sat back in a recliner at home, watching recorded episodes of "The Great Race" for about a half hour at a time and dozing off for another half hour or so, back and forth. I wasn't really sick, but I was unwell enough to feel not the least bit guilty for lounging in front of the TV for two days.

A week later I drove myself to Fort Collins to have the stitches removed. I expected the doctor to snip each loop, but she just snipped the end and pulled the thread through. It was an odd sensation. The result was worth it, I think. It made me more wide-eyed than sleepy-eyed even if it did move parts of my eyebrows where they don't belong. I don't know that it made me any more feminine-looking, but it did improve my looks a bit.

In my attempt to understand this disconnect between my body and my inner being I'd read whatever I could find through the years. I'd read clinical papers and magazine articles and essays and autobiographies. Someone on the internet forum recommended a new book: *True Selves*.[1] The library didn't have a copy, so I bought one and read it through. I found this to be the best explanation that I'd yet encountered of what was going on with me. I ordered a dozen copies and gave them to my daughter, sister, brother, minister, friends, and the library at the university's LGBT office. I don't know if anyone read it, but in a way it was a gesture that said: "Here. This is me."

Come January, I drove to Florida to visit my Rhode Island friends Dan and Steve at their winter home. To get there while avoiding as much bad weather as possible, I would have to go through Colorado, Texas, Louisiana, Mississippi, Alabama, and Georgia. I had been through the area several times before and usually was not comfortable in the Deep South. As Kate for less than a year and, I thought, easily identifiable as trans, I didn't know what to expect. I remembered signs at the highway rest areas proclaiming that they were patrolled 24-hours a day. Rather than feeling reassured, to me the signs implied a certain lawlessness. Why else would they feel the need to post them?

The bathroom wars had begun, with people taking it upon themselves to keep those predatory transgender people out of the ladies' rooms. I was still legally male – it said so on my driver's license. I was still physically male, mostly. I'd lived in many parts of the country but never in the Deep South. Most of what I knew of the region was from books and movies, and much of that was not flattering. I could easily picture an encounter with a right-eously outraged proper Southern woman calling Sheriff Bubba to protect her from me. I went anyway.

That January was unusually cold in the South. There was snow and ice and freezing temperatures in northern Mississippi and Alabama. Reasoning that the drivers in that area would be unused to dealing with those conditions, I went farther south than I had planned, along the Gulf Coast. But I angled up though Montgomery to Atlanta. I wanted to visit my brother in North Carolina to show him his new sister.

I had never been in the roadside women's restrooms on that route. In Alabama I went into one with flowers pictured in the tiles. This did seem to be a foreign land; the extra expense of the flowered tiles seemed to say to me that women were special, as long as they knew their place. I didn't encounter any outraged proper Southern ladies, though.

From Atlanta, I drove north to Asheville, North Carolina. I wanted to visit the memorial garden at the Unitarian Universalist church where my parents' ashes are. I hadn't been there since my father's memorial service, eighteen years before. I wanted to show them that their troubled and troublesome third child, who could never quite find himself, had turned out all right.

The memorial garden had become more of one since I was last there. When I had last seen it, it had been just a small tree with ground cover around it. Now it was planted with other things, had brass plaques and benches, and was enclosed by a privacy fence. It was simple but very nicely done. I entered the enclosure, read the plaques, sat down, and surprising myself, I began to cry. I was just so terribly sad that I hadn't managed to get my act together during their lifetimes. I think that they had never quite managed to figure me out, and they didn't understand why I struggled so long to find my place in the world. If I had managed to become Kate while they were still alive, I imagine they would have said, "Oh. Now we get it."

It was insanely cold for North Carolina: 17°. I sat for about half an hour, until I got so chilled that I had to leave.

I drove down from the mountains to the Piedmont to visit my brother. His reaction to my coming out letter was one of guarded acceptance. He didn't understand, and I think he had the feeling that this might be just one more crazy scheme I'd come up with. He was worried about the speed of my transition and about my scheduled surgery. He didn't want me hurt. He didn't want me to back myself into a corner from which I wouldn't be able to recover.

We had a long talk, and I gave him a copy of *True Selves*. He asked how common it was to be transgender. I told him that I knew of no reliable data, but the estimate that seemed most accurate to me because of how it was derived put the incidence between one in 100 to 200 births – about half as likely as having naturally red hair. I was a little surprised that even though he was a college professor like my neighbor Steve, he seemed to have so little awareness of transgender people. He did introduce me to one of his neighbors as his sister, though.

From his house I went to Savannah and then to Dan and Steve's home in Fort Myers. Dan's sister Arlene and her husband had rented a nearby condo for the month. I stayed five days, much of the time with the four of them. I had met Arlene before but didn't know her well. She was glad I was there, because I was happy to go clothes shopping with her. Her husband wouldn't go, and Dan and Steve, she said, were useless in that regard.

The cold snap had embraced all of Florida, too, so it was too cold to go to the beach. Arlene and I happily cruised the shops instead. I found an inexpensive bathing suit with a skirt that hid my narrow hips and the unfortunate accessories below.

Leaving Florida, I drove the direct route home. The snow in the Southeast had turned to rain, so I could travel back home by a more northern route. I stopped in Nashville to see where The Grand Ol' Opry is held and in Paducah, Kentucky, to look at the National Quilt Museum, but otherwise I just drove through the cold rain, covering the 2,100 miles in four days.

When I was young, my grandmother had trained me in some of the old-fashioned chivalrous acts – hold doors open for women, walk on the gutter side of the sidewalk, and so on. On this trip I was delighted that there were times when men would hold a door open for me. It took a few times for me to return the courtesy by accepting their gesture with a smile and genuine "thank you."

My confidence increased. I had driven over 4,000 miles with no problems, no scares. The only odd point came when I stopped at a convenience store in a poor neighborhood in West Baton Rouge, and that was only because it was *very* obvious I wasn't from around there and didn't belong there. Across the country, everyone accepted me as a woman, even if a few might have recognized me as transgender. Pleased with myself, I reported to the Fort Collins support group that everyone across the country had seen me as a woman.

14

BECOMING ✳ 2010

"Often, it's not about becoming a new person, but becoming the person you were meant to be, and already are, but don't know how to be."
— Heath L. Buckmaster, *Box of Hair: A Fairy Tale*

Part of the protocol for getting GRS was to have letters from two psychiatrists or PhD psychologists saying, essentially, I wasn't crazy for wanting the surgery. Actually, the letters were to state why surgery was the right treatment.

There were ways to shortcut the process – not do the full year of living full-time and shopping around to find someone to provide a letter with only a cursory analysis. To me, that was cheating – cheating the system and cheating yourself. I had met someone who had done it that way. She was having trouble with her new status – it wasn't how she'd pictured it. It was too bad, but I felt that she had brought it on herself.

I was still in counseling with Judith, who'd helped me through Polly's decline and death. She would give me one letter, but I needed another. I asked a psychologist I knew at church. She was heavily involved in something and didn't think she had the time to do it right. I needed letters a month before my surgery and couldn't wait for her.

I asked a woman I knew only slightly from the few times she had come to the church. She agreed to do it but insisted on at least eight sessions. To me, the letter was a given, but she felt that to ethically provide it she needed the time with me. I agreed. As we started the sessions, our relationship shifted from friendly acquaintances to counselor-client. I was interested to see this other side of her.

When I got the two letters, Judith's was very thorough. She'd counseled me for years. Even so, I was surprised at how well she knew me. Ann's letter was shorter, not as extensive or as deeply knowing of me. Both letters stated the opinion that I would be successful living as a woman. I hadn't thought of that, but of course it was an important judgment. The surgery is irreversible. The surgeon wants to help me, not make my life worse.

When I told my friend Bruce that I was going to have surgery, he complained. "But when you started this, you said you weren't going to become a woman!" I replied, palms upraised, "That just goes to show how little I knew at the time." He had no problem with it; he just hadn't been expecting it. And I think that was true for most of my friends. They were just watching to see where I was going with this.

As the anniversary of my coming out at church approached, Penny and I started planning something to mark the occasion. Because Easter moves with the lunar as well as the solar calendar, the anniversary would not be Easter but on the Sunday after. I wanted something modeled on the bridging ceremony girls have when they move from Brownies to Girl Scouts. I had never been either a Brownie or a Girl Scout but liked the idea as a way to mark moving from one phase of your life to the next.

I had recently been exposed to some of Margaret Fuller's life and writings. Under the very strict tutelage of her father, she had become an intellectual and social activist in the 1800s – a time when women generally weren't thought worthy of education. She had received a remarkable classical education but one without feeling. Upon her father's death, she became free to explore this other aspect of her nature. She fell in love and married. In short, she had lived one constricted life of the mind and then moved into a life that included the freedom to have emotions. In some ways, her story resonated with me.

Upon marrying, Fuller was still an intellectual powerhouse. We carry our past with us as we evolve. In my simpler, much less elevated life, I was the same person I had been, but freer and expanded.

Penny and I decided to do the bridging ceremony at the end of the Candles of Joys and Concerns. I joined her at the front, and my friends Jim and Sharon joined us. Penny explained a little of Margaret Fuller's background and quoted what Fuller wrote to a friend once she had started living more freely:

"I can say very little now, scarce a word that is not absolutely drawn from me at the moment. I cannot plunge into myself enough. I cannot dedicate myself sufficiently. The life that glows in upon me from so many quarters is too beautiful to be checked. I would not check a single pulsation. It all ought to be... My soul swells with the future. The past, I know it not...

"Truly you say I have not been what I am now yet it is only transformation, not alteration. The leaf became a stem, a bud, is now a flower..."

I continued the quote:

"Trapped by expectations

I kept the best of me hidden

And shushed her when she spoke."

Then Jim spoke: "Go, my brother. Seek what we all seek – happiness, wholeness, and wisdom."

And Sharon: "Welcome, my sister. Enter the tribe of your soul. Relax and take comfort."

Wrapping up, I lit a candle and spoke again:

"A year ago I lit a candle in joy for this gathering of kind and generous souls – you, who have created a sanctuary where I could finally dare to hope.

"I announced that I was starting a journey to find myself, to let the cage door swing open and free myself if I could.

"I shed the mask I felt obligated to wear – obligated by my anatomy and by social expectations. With your kindness, and the kindness of others, I have not had to put on a new mask but can reveal myself – my only true self.

"I have been like a desert flower, parched, held tight against the heat and the cold, waiting.

"Your open minds and open hearts have been like the long-awaited rain, allowing me to bloom at last.

"And that gives me such joy that I should light a whole tray of candles."

As I went back to my seat, Penny said, "After the service Kate will sign the membership book again – this time as her true self."

The responses after the service were positive and many. A woman I had become friendly with and who had come to the church for the first time the previous Easter, when I had come out, told me, "*That's* why I come to this church!"

It was yet another amazing day.

As I got closer to my surgery date, I became more and more excited. I hadn't dared to hope; I hadn't known what I wanted; I hadn't thought that I needed it. But now I was certain: I wanted this more than I'd wanted anything. I steeled myself for disappointment, but it kept looking like it would finally happen. I worried that there would be a glitch, something out of my control. The surgeon would fall ill. Or maybe some crazy person would blow up the hospital. Or maybe a giant meteor would hit southern Colorado. If some crazy person did blow up the hospital, I hoped they'd wait until after my surgery, even if I was still there. I was really focused on this one thing.

I was focused, but it was a weird time. One morning in the shower I found myself talking to my boy bits, reassuring them I was not mad at them and wouldn't get rid of them – they would just be rearranged. And I knew that it would hurt because they would be cut and sewn, but in the long run we would all be happier with the new configuration.

I sent in the paperwork. I gathered the things the surgeon's office staff said I'd need, augmented by advice on the forum. I got a certified check for the balance due before the surgery could start.

I made arrangements to get to Trinidad and home again. Jody, my laser tech, offered to drive me. That seemed above and beyond to me, and I was touched by the offer. I doubt that she offered it to all of her transgender clients. I could drive myself, but it might be difficult driving back home after the surgery. One of the effects of the surgery would be that sitting would be difficult, especially for any length of time. And the acts of sitting down and getting back up would be difficult, too.

I arranged with friends to drive me to my sister's, north of Denver, and pick me up again on the return trip. I would stay overnight at my sister's on the way south. Without my asking, brother-in-law Joe volunteered to drive me to Trinidad and stay with me through the surgery. Casey would fly to Denver and drive to Trinidad to stay with me the rest of the time. She would drive me back to Joe's. Because my car was pretty low, had firm seats, and had a manual transmission that Casey couldn't drive, I reserved a large Chevrolet rental car, with high, soft seats and an automatic transmission. Joe and I would pick it up for the trip south, Joe would drive it home and turn it over to Casey, and she would turn it in when she drove me back. It was all set.

The Sunday before I was to leave for Trinidad, I said my goodbyes at church, in person and to the congregation during Candles.

"I light a candle this morning in joy for this gathering of kind and generous souls. Your open minds and open hearts have made it possible for me to become myself. I leave Tuesday for another step in my journey. I will be gone two weeks and will return home to an indefinite period of recovery. I go in joy and will return in celebration."

I was ready, eager. There was no reason to think that there might be a problem, but even if it killed me or drastically shortened my life, I was going to do it. The only known death was a person who'd had the genital surgery, breast implants, and facial reconstruction all done at the same time. Her body just couldn't handle the combined assaults on it.

I did add a bit of surgery for appearances, though. I opted for a tracheal shave, to remove the bulge of my Adam's apple. It was a common add-on and shouldn't be a problem. I'd read some discussions about the tracheal shave. It was a minor operation, but if something went wrong it could affect your voice or perhaps even your ability to swallow. I wanted it done by someone who knew what they were doing and who had a lot of experience.

Penny said she would be driving from Laramie to her home in Boulder on Tuesday morning and that she would be happy to take me as far as my sister's house. Tuesday morning I met her for breakfast at a diner in downtown Laramie, and we set off on the first leg of the journey.

Wednesday morning, Joe and I picked up the rental car, and he drove us to Trinidad. We checked into the guest/recovery house where I would stay before the surgery and after being released from the hospital. It was a large, old house that had been divided up for its new use. There was one separate apartment on the ground floor, but the rest were rooms with a shared bathroom and a shared common area on each of the two floors. There was also a shared kitchen for our use. I think the house could accommodate seven or eight guests. While I was there, all the other guests were male-to-female transsexuals, either waiting for surgery or recovering from it. Joe and I checked into two rooms on the second floor and then went to a recommended restaurant for supper. It would be my last decent meal for a while.

Thursday morning I met with the surgeon for the first time. She did more than 200 of these operations each year and had been doing them for ten or fifteen years. She assured me all would be well. I began the bowel prep in the afternoon. I wasn't to eat anything after noon and wasn't even to have water or brush my teeth after 6 PM. It was OK because at that point I would do anything to make this happen.

Fortunately, my surgery was scheduled for the morning rather than afternoon. Friday morning, Joe took me to the hospital at 5 AM. I met with the surgeon again. She carefully marked my neck so the incision for the tracheal shave would fall on a wrinkle and be less noticeable. The anesthesiologist introduced himself. And it all began.

I had a pretty good idea of what would be done, how it all would be reconfigured and what existing tissue would be used for what in the new setup. Some months later I came across a YouTube video of the procedure. Yowch! No wonder it hurt so much afterward. I was glad I hadn't seen the video beforehand – I would have been even more anxious. The basic idea was to use the skin of the penis to form a vagina inside me and use some of the other tissue to form labia. The urethra would be shortened and rerouted. The muscles across the pelvic floor would be pushed aside for the vaginal vestibule. And the testicles would be discarded, consigned to the fiery furnace of hell as far as I was concerned.

I remember half-waking and trying to get them to tell me they had done it, but they must have sedated me again. I probably sounded delirious. I woke again, slowly, in the recovery room. Joe was there. My first words were, "Did they do it?" Even then I was still afraid I'd be denied my dream.

Joe assured me that they had, indeed, done it, and that the surgeon said it had gone very well. The surgery had taken four hours. Joe and I talked for a long time. Then he went off for supper and I drifted back to sleep.

I woke in a single room in the hospital. I had an IV and an assortment of tubes and drains in me, immobilizing me. But I was too weak to go anywhere anyway. The surgeon came by to tell me what a wonderful job she'd done. Joe came back for a while. Nurses were in and out. They told me not to chase my pain, so when it intensified and seemed like it wasn't going to level off, I asked for a painkiller. They gave me Percocet. I'll never take another. I know that for some people, Percocet barely knocks the edge off the pain, but for me it gave me a night I hope to never repeat. It was almost an out-of-body experience, one filled with vivid, almost surreal hallucinations, while my body was immobilized and incapable of feeling. When I mentioned my frightening night to a nurse the next morning, she said, "Oh, so you had the dreams, huh?" Evidently I'm not the only one that Percocet affects in this way.

Joe visited me several times on Saturday as I drifted in and out of sleep, still hooked up to all sorts of tubes and drains. That night as the pain built, they again offered me Percocet, but I refused. After checking with the doctor, they gave me Darvocet, which worked for me.

The next morning, Sunday, they began unhooking me from most of my tethers. Freed, I began feeling almost human even though I was sore, weak, and very tired. The nurses encouraged me to stand up, and I tried. But the muscles across my pelvic floor that had been repositioned during the surgery weren't cooperative, and I fell back onto the bed.

They said I should rest and they would come back in the afternoon to try again. Being able to walk was important – I wouldn't be released from the hospital until I could do that. Looking out my door, I could see the woman from the guest house who'd been operated on the afternoon after me, chugging up and down the hall. I was determined to walk that afternoon.

When the nurses came back after lunch for another try, with their help I was able to stand. I walked gingerly to the chair next to the bed. Soon I had the strength to walk the halls, too. It was good to be able to get myself to the bathroom, wash up, and brush my teeth. I realized that when your world gets to be the size of a hospital room, your goals get pretty small.

Joe visited me several times on Sunday. On Monday morning, he stuck his head in and said goodbye. He was going to drive back home in the falling rain and snow. He would pick up Casey when she flew into Denver the next day. I spent the rest of Monday walking up and down the hospital hallways, determined to rebuild my strength.

Late Tuesday morning I was released from the hospital and driven to the guest house. I was given several prescriptions, one of which was for Percocet. I gave that one back to them. As it turned out, once out of the hospital I never took any pain-killer stronger than aspirin, and not very many of them. I was overwhelmed by the pain in the beginning, but I was amazed at how quickly it subsided into only discomfort.

I spent the rest of that day alone in my room but had dinner that evening with the other guests. Casey arrived Wednesday afternoon after driving the rental car from Marty and Joe's house. We shared a large room in the back of the second floor. The only other inhabitant on that floor was a tiny Laotian-born nurse from Texas. She kept to her room and we rarely saw her, so we had the upstairs common room pretty much to ourselves.

Casey had originally wanted to stay with me for a week after I got back to Laramie, but I asked her to come to Trinidad instead. There were friends in Laramie I could rely on if needed. I thought I'd need her support more in Trinidad. And, as it worked out, her presence and patience with me was very, very welcome. Once out of the hospital I could walk short distances and get around, but I was very glad to not have to drive. And our talks and short excursions were wonderful. It was a little crazy at the guest house, with all of us recovering from long yearned-for surgery but with very little else in common. Casey's presence brought a much-needed normalcy as I continued to heal.

On Thursday, six days after my surgery, Casey drove me back to the hospital to have the surgical dressings removed. I also got a lesson on caring for the new arrangement – what most girls learn early in their lives but was new to me. On the internet forum, someone from England posted that to get the surgery in that country you had to sign a paper acknowledging that after the surgery you would have to sit to pee. I think my surgeon mentioned this to me, too. It seems obvious, but perhaps some people don't think it through.

In the car after visiting the hospital, with Casey driving me to the Social Security office to change my gender marker, I burst into tears. It just came over me. I was a mess – deep, wracking sobs. I had never cried like that before. I was just so happy, so relieved. It was a core-deep, down-in-my-soul happiness that is beyond my description. Whatever pain I had suffered in the previous 66 years didn't count, because I was finally OK.

This transformation that I thought could never happen, that I thought somehow wouldn't happen, that I dared not hope for, that I had wanted all my life but knew was impossible, that I denied I wanted and needed – this amazing, life-changing, wonderful change had been accomplished and, however things worked out in the future, for now I was OK. I was more OK than I had ever been.

Once the pain from the surgery had subsided and the dressing removed I felt a calm peace, the depth of which surprised me. I'd thought of the external aspects – the look, the legal and social implications – but had not considered what it would feel like inside. I now had this small space inside me that should have always been there. I had a small cavity instead of the weight of the unwanted male genitals. I didn't understand how I could know so deeply that this was right. I could only sigh: How wonderful. I've gotten used to it, of course, and hardly ever think of it, but the difference was very noticeable at first.

Most of the women at the guest house were alone. One woman had a post-op transsexual friend with her, and the tiny Laotian-born nurse from Texas had been adopted by some of the local hospital nurses, but I was the only one with family. Flowers from the church had been delivered to me at the hospital. To my surprise, on Thursday I got flowers from Judith, my counselor, at the guest house. Then on Friday, when a card came for me in the mail, the woman who ran the house said in a mocking, sing-song voice, "No one gets flowers, but Kate gets flowers. No one gets cards, but Kate gets cards." I was sorry most of the others had to go through this alone, but I was pleased to get the flowers and cards. And accompanied by Joe and then Casey, I felt absolutely and thoroughly blessed.

Monday morning, ten days after surgery, I was given the OK to leave Trinidad. Casey and I set off north to my sister's house. We had to stop several times for me to walk around – the hours of sitting were difficult – but I was glad to be in a car and not confined to an airplane seat. My Laramie friend Sarah was waiting for me, and she drove me the rest of the way. Casey stayed in Colorado to turn in the car and fly home. When I got home I found that Sarah and other friends had stocked my refrigerator.

Back home in Laramie, I was healed enough to be able to take care of myself. Friends brought meals for me, but on my first full day at home I drove myself to the a nearby school to vote in the primary election. It would be a few weeks before I could drive as far as Fort Collins, and another three months before I dared to ride the motorcycle, but I was fine driving short hops around town. My trip to Trinidad had been two weeks. Two weeks to get reconfigured and heal enough to care for myself again. Two weeks to make it possible for me to change the gender marker on my driver's license, Medicare card, passport, birth certificate, conceal carry permit, and, yes, my voter registration. A necessary two weeks. I was on a high just being able to go have the surgery, and some of the trip to Trinidad was good, but my memory of it is of a difficult two weeks made much, much easier by the love and support of those close to me.

In the dream, I am standing on the side of a city street. There are no sidewalks and the grimy grey buildings crowd the edges of the pavement. Overhead are elevated train tracks, filling the space between the buildings. The overhead tracks are supported by iron posts reinforced with latticework. They are old and black and dirty. It is dark, the streetlights are dim in the gloom, and there are deep shadows. Ahead of me is an intersection with five streets entering at odd angles. Some of the posts supporting the el tracks are in the middle of the street. The scene is from years ago, out of Dickens or perhaps film noir. The street surface looks like it is a mix of brick and cobblestones. Embedded in the pavement are a network of train tracks willy-nilly, crossing each other at odd angles and curving off around the corners and into the distance, almost like a plate of spaghetti noodles. Steam trains and old streetcars appear suddenly out of the gloom, from around a corner or behind me. It amazes me that they don't run into each other as they pass at almost cartoonish speed. I am trying to get to the corner, but I have to cross some of the tracks to get there. I keep looking about me, hoping to be able to see a train and figure out which track it is following before it gets close. I am not scared; I am careful, wary, alert, cautious. I take a step and wake up.

I'd had this dream for as long as I can remember. I might go several years without it, but then I'd have it again. The dream was always the same, the feeling was always the same. The tangle of tracks through the space in front of me was always the same. In the dream, trains zip by, but I don't know which of the rails in the tangle will be the ones they'll use. Sometimes in the dream I can take several tentative steps and sometimes only one, but I always wake up before I get very far.

After I had come out to my friends, I had the dream again. This time, though, the setting was different, almost like something from a western movie.

I am standing on an open plain of golden-green prairie grass. The sun is bright in a clear sky. I am facing two sets of railroad tracks that head off straight to the horizon to my right and left. On the other side of the tracks the land rises in a gentle, grassy slope. There is no one around, and the only things I can see from horizon to horizon are the railroad tracks and the grass of the wide-open prairie. I am trying to get to the slope on the other side of the tracks. I step carefully forward, almost to the first rail. I wake up.

I knew it was the same dream despite the differences – it was open and very bright, and the tracks were straight. This time there were no trains in the dream – just the empty tracks. I was puzzled that it was the same dream but that there were just two sets of tracks and that they were straight. I wondered if it meant something.

A few months later, I had the dream one more time. Again the setting was different, but I knew it was the same dream.

I am standing in tall, green grass, with some leafy trees off to my side. I am facing just a single set of railroad tracks. On the other side are some blank-faced buildings at the railroad's edge. The tracks run off to my right and left. In front of my feet is a rustic crossing with wooden boards laid between the tracks, level with the tops of the rails, like something you would drive a wagon across. There's no train. I step forward onto the wooden crossing – one step, then another, and another. I am across the tracks, standing between the buildings. There are a series of doors on either side of me. I wonder what I should do next, but I am not anxious, just curious. I wake up.

Awake, I realized with some surprise that this was the first time I'd gotten across the tracks. I haven't had the dream since.

I think that for most people, Transition – the period of moving from presenting as one gender to living as your true self – ends with surgery, or so they think. I found that I still had a lot of transitioning to do. I had changed my name, my hormones, my clothes, and my body; but I was still learning to be Kate. It wasn't just my body or the social conventions. Despite wanting it my whole life, I didn't have much experience being a woman in the world.

Transitioning was very public in a small town like Laramie, which had a population of about 27,000 at the time. It wasn't just my friends and neighbors who knew. It seemed like the whole town knew what I was doing. In the beginning I looked very much like I had except one day I began wearing women's clothes. Even those who didn't know me but remembered me from yesterday or last week could see what was happening. The transformation didn't happen overnight, and surgery didn't complete the process. I still had a lot of work to do.

The first time that I was talking and a man started talking over me, it took a minute for me to realize what was happening. I knew men did this to women, but knowing something and experiencing it are not the same thing. The transition to living as a woman continues.

I had come to think of the male me and the female me as two distinct people even though I always knew they were both aspects of me. Through much of my life the male me had hidden, even denied, the presence of the female me – hidden sometimes even from myself. Giving her a name – Katherine – had been a first step. My women's clothes had become Katherine clothes. As I told people about this female me, she became more real to me. Sitting in a coffee shop as the old, male me I would write in my diary that it was time to go home to see what Katherine was up to. Then I would go home and put on my Katherine clothes and putter around the house. The female me emerged more and more. It was a rapid but gradual blossoming of the female me that had always been there, hidden away. Now that the female me could live openly, it was time to let the male me go away.

One evening I got a phone call soliciting for something. The young woman asked for me by my old name. For some reason, I replied sadly, "He's gone." She seemed alarmed. "Oh! Has he died?" Still with my sad voice, I said, "No. He's just gone." She said she was very sorry and that she would remove him from her list.

I wasn't making it up. I had come to think of my former self as "him" and that he had moved away, to Nebraska or someplace. I had no ill feelings and wished him well, but I didn't want to see him again.

I was ready to move on to my life as Kate. But first I needed to reconcile with my old self, so I wrote him a letter:

Hi Dan. It's me, Katherine. I ... I know I've been ignoring you. OK, I'll admit there have been times when I pretended you never existed. But it's not that I want to forget you, or that I have any ill feeling toward you. It's just that I really need to establish my own life, and – well, sometimes it's easier if I act as if you'd never been.

Listen, I want to let you know how much I appreciate you keeping me safe all those years – through the school locker rooms, and the Army, and when we went down those dark alleys and lived, too often, in those sketchy neighborhoods. It's true that we got beat up that time, walking home from school. I'm sorry. Thank goodness the violin didn't get broken. That – and the other times we were attacked – was probably 'cause people could see me a little, making you look like an easy victim. But that time we were mugged while standing at the urinal in junior high wasn't my fault. That was just a tough school.

Hah! Remember those times when I would say something and some guy would look at you like: What planet are you from? He expected you to be from Mars, like him, but we had roots in Venus, despite appearances. I know those times were embarrassing for you, but I thought they were funny. It made things tough on you, I know, but we did all right.

Really, I want you to know how much I appreciate you getting me strong enough to show myself to the world. It took a long time before I dared. I'm such a coward. Thank you for nurturing me until I could come out. That first time, talking to your friends about me was scary, but it turned out well. They're nice people. Remember: they were your friends first.

I really needed those hormone treatments. That's when you started to let me live, and I thank you for that. You have to admit, though, you were always troubled with the setup before then – I guess because I was hiding there within you.

Living out in the world, with people who had known you and were getting to know me, was quite an adventure, wasn't it? It was scary but so much fun. We did OK, didn't we?

And then the surgery. You were gone then, letting me blossom into the woman I needed to be. Wow. Who knew how wonderful life would be for me? I can be present in the world now, after all those years of hiding. Now it's my name on the driver's license instead of yours.

But I will always carry you within me, just as you always carried me within you. We're a funny mix, huh? Our life is so much better now that I can be the face the world sees, but I don't blame you for that. Sometimes I pretend you had never been, but I know I wouldn't have gotten here without you.

Thanks Dan.

15

GROWING ✳ 2011-2012

"You can't grow if you are afraid of change."
— Bernardo Moya

Life was perfect. I was Kate. I was accepted as a woman – or at least the woman that I am. I had friends who loved me and neighbors who accepted me. I had a little house in a beautiful part of the world. I had a job – treasurer of the UU Fellowship – that gave me something to do and a way to earn the respect of others. Life was good. Very good.

But my daughter lived 1,200 miles away. I would drive out to see her now and then, but I wanted to be closer. The Wyoming winters made me restless, and I would start planning trips for the summer. During the winter of 2010-11, I began thinking of moving to the Pacific Northwest. I'd been in Laramie nine years – longer than I'd lived anywhere as an adult.

I looked online for places in northwest Washington – Seattle, Tacoma, Olympia, the Olympic Peninsula. Nothing looked right. I didn't know what I wanted – I wasn't ready to move anyway – but I couldn't picture myself (my new self) as living in any of those places.

Then someone suggested Portland. I'd been through Portland dozens of times but had never actually been in the city. I felt some urgency to go look. I knew it could be beautiful in the summer and wanted to see it while it was still grey and wet. Having lived in Seattle, I knew it could be grey and wet a *lot*.

I thought if I was going to move to a city, I wanted to live in the city itself. I found ten condos online that were in my price range and arranged with a realtor to show them to me. I hadn't been on an airplane in ten years – since before 9/11 – but I bought a ticket. Joe, who had driven me to Trinidad, drove me to the airport. And off I went.

Portland completely seduced me. It rained half the time I was there, but I loved every minute.

Some of the condos were wrong for me and some were OK, but in one of them I could hear a voice within me: "This is where you belong, Katherine." It was quite distinct. I don't usually hear voices. In fact I don't remember ever having heard one before. I might have inklings of danger sometimes, and I might even heed those warnings, sometimes. But this was different.

I liked the place and it seemed like a good fit. I didn't intend to move for another year or two, but this condo really drew me to it. I went back for a second look. And again for a third one. I began to see it realistically, without the gauzy surprise of my first visit. Still, it would work for me. I could see myself living there. To break the spell, I went back to Laramie, but Portland and the condo still pulled me. I put in an offer, and after some negotiating I agreed to buy it. Then came the scramble to sell my Laramie house and untangle from my connections there.

The realtor who'd sold me my house ten years earlier helped me get it ready even though she'd known me in a different guise. It all worked out like it was meant to be, and maybe it was. I said goodbye to the people who'd helped me and encouraged me and supported me on my journey to wholeness. The movers came to load their truck, and I drove out to Olympia to attend Casey's wedding as one of the mothers of the bride. (That was a fun time. I had known some of Casey's friends for years. And Valerie's sister and step-mother were there, seeing me as Kate for the first time. It was a lovely wedding and a lovely weekend.)

Then I drove to my new home and began settling in. I moved to Portland knowing no one. My move to Laramie had been the first time I'd moved because I wanted to – not for a job or for school – but Polly and I had done it together. Moving to Portland was mine and mine alone. Perhaps part of the reason for doing it was to prove to myself that I could.

In Laramie I had tended Polly as she declined into death. Then, after a lifetime of waiting, I had transitioned to living as Kate. To *being* Kate. Now, moving to a very different home in a very different place while knowing no one, I was starting my new life my new life as Kate. I was ready.

I had been very involved in the UU fellowship in Laramie. The people there had been invaluable to me during Polly's decline and then again through my transition to living openly as Kate. I had met most of my Laramie friends at the fellowship, but it was a small congregation of about 50 members. The Portland area has eight UU churches or fellowships. I thought I might have to go to one of the smaller ones, like the one in Laramie, but the closest to my new home was the big one downtown, with over 1,000 members. I'd try that one first.

As I met people I didn't hide the fact that I am transsexual, but I avoided mentioning it as best I could. It wasn't from fear or embarrassment, but I didn't want to deflect our conversation to that aspect of me. I wanted to establish myself as Kate, not Kate-who-used-to-live-as-a-man. And being Kate out in the world was still new to me. I needed to make her more solid.

In Laramie, my transition had been very public. In Portland I was enjoying the anonymity of the big city. Whether people recognized that I am transgender or not, they just treated me as Kate, this new woman living in The Pearl. I loved it. I loved my new life.

I continued going to the downtown church. I loved the music and the services and that it offered lots of classes and activities. And yes, I loved the convenience – being able to walk there if I wanted. Knowing no one, I went into active friend-seeking mode. This was new behavior for me. Much of my life I had tried to be invisible, to stay in the background, simultaneously hoping someone would notice me and that no one would.

I signed up for classes and workshops, volunteered as an usher, and spent the social hours after the service talking to anyone who would talk to me. It was a friendly place, and I felt comfortable there. I refused no invitations. I met a woman who had moved from New York and lived in the condo two doors down from mine. Zoe was a Unitarian too, and she joined the same women's circle as I had. We went to the symphony together. She became a good friend.

Then, one Sunday during the social hour after church, I met a tall, good-looking woman. I was attracted to her bearing and her self-possession. She seemed comfortable with herself, comfortable in this space. I thought: If I can be this woman's friend....

I continued the morning walks I'd begun in Laramie, enjoying my new city before it was fully awake. I got in the habit of stopping for coffee on the way back. One morning, I was feeling weak and turned around about halfway through my walk. By the time I got my coffee, I felt like I was going to collapse. I was alarmed enough to call 911. An ambulance came and took me to the hospital, where I stayed for two days while they ran me through all sorts of tests. The presenting problem was that I had atrial fibrillation – a-fib.

There were two outcomes of this episode. The first was that they put me on a medication that, while it controlled the a-fib, affected my sense of balance. I could walk all right, but if I stood still, I would soon need to touch something steady – a lamppost, or the person I was talking to. It made riding the motorcycle really scary. After a few months they put me on a different medication, but the damage had been done. I never regained my confidence riding the bike. I'd loved motorcycling and it had done a lot to make me the confident person I'd finally become, but I knew that phase of my life was over. It was all right, though, because I was building this wonderful new life.

The other result of the hospital sojourn was that I was now connected into the medical system. When I met my general practitioner, my first words were, "I'm transgender, and if you have a problem with that, tell me now." I had read too many stories on the forum about medical professionals treating transgender people with disrespect and callousness, even treating them as subhuman. It had taken me too long to get where I was and I wasn't going to put up with a professional raising their eyebrows at me. But she dismissed my concerns as not relevant. Evidently there had been a lot of progress in the profession, or at least in Portland.

Sundays, I continued meeting people at church. Sometimes I would see the tall, attractive woman I'd met there – Andrea – and sometimes she would invite me to a choral concert or to tea. We were slowly becoming friends. I was happy to spend time with her, but our budding friendship was just a small part of this new, wonderful life. Health issues aside, I was happier than I thought was possible. I was living a life I had never expected, more wonderful than I had ever dreamed. I was beyond happy.

In mid-December, Andrea invited me to her birthday party. There I met three of her girlfriends, and the five of us drank White Russians and sang Christmas carols late into the night. The next day I had lunch with another woman from the church, then met Andrea for supper at my favorite pub. We sat together happily, talking about the party and this and that. After supper, I asked if she'd like to see my apartment. She agreed, and we walked there and talked more. Then, because it was late, I drove her home. I pulled up across from her condo, blocking the post office driveway. But the post office was closed, and I expected Andrea to say goodnight and go into her building. But she showed no signs of getting out.

We turned to each other in the darkened car and continued to talk. It had been a nice evening, and we were easy with each other. I was relaxed, happy to extend our time together. After a while, she paused and said, "It is my sense that you were born into a male body." I was a little surprised. She'd never given the slightest indication that she knew I am transgender. And I liked how she said it – that this was the way I was born. Feeling safe with her, I told her my story.

Andrea is a good listener. She sat quietly, without judgment, letting me talk, open to whatever I wished to say. It was considerably later when I finally stopped.

It was good to tell someone. The world was unchanged – we were still sitting in the darkened car, still parked across the post office driveway, the city still asleep – but something had shifted. Inside the car, we were as we had been, still new friends, sitting turned to each other across the car, getting to know each other. But I was lighter now. I had told Andrea things I had told no one else. I felt more free, more open. It was a good feeling.

We had been sitting in the car for almost two hours, but Andrea still showed no sign of getting out and going into her building. We sat there a while longer, quiet in our deepened relationship.

Then she said, "I have something to tell you. Remember when

we sat together at church?" We'd sat together only once, earlier that month. She sang in the choir and I was an usher, so we hadn't had much opportunity to sit together. She continued, "When we were singing 'Spirit of Life' your voice dropped into its natural, lower voice. I felt my heart pop open – a physical sensation. And I realized: I've just fallen in love with this woman. I love you Kate."

I sat stunned. Andrea – lovely, sweet, competent and confident Andrea – was saying she loved me. How could this be? She'd always been with men, had always been attracted to men. She was opening a door to possibilities I had no idea even existed.

I said, "But you've always been with men!" And she replied, "I know. And now I've fallen in love with a woman. A transgender woman." Still confused, I said, "And old." She smiled, "An old transgender woman."

I was dumbstruck. I couldn't get my bearings. All I could think was: Don't screw this up. Afraid of saying the wrong thing, I just sat there. Andrea asked, "Do you think you could love me?"

I couldn't say anything. I was too amazed, flabbergasted. My brain had stopped working.

Finally, Andrea reached for the door handle, wished me good night, and walked into her building. Somehow, I managed to drive home.

I had been living the perfect life. I was Kate at last. I had moved to a beautiful condo in a wonderful neighborhood in Portland. I was happier than I had ever been – happier than I had ever hoped to be. Life couldn't get any better.

But then, here was Andrea. She was such a lovely, friendly, smart, competent person. I began to suspect that perhaps she wasn't real. Perhaps she was an angel sent, for some odd reason, to make my life even more perfect. I didn't believe in such things as angels, but what other explanation could there be? Her falling in love with me was beyond possible, beyond imagining.

Really, the whole thing was preposterous. I was 68 years old and building a new life as Kate. I had a lifetime of needing to be Kate but being afraid of that need. I was just getting my life on track and had no expectations of making room for anyone else. Andrea had always been with men and was, besides that, above my touch. That she had admitted me into her circle of friends was a gift in itself. I expected nothing more.

But she was offering me more. She opened the door to love, and I cautiously stepped in. We began spending more time together – a lot more time. Several days after her declaration of love, we had supper at my condo and spent the evening talking. One thing led to another, and we ended up in the bedroom. I hadn't been with anyone since my surgery, but it didn't seem to make any difference. Overwhelmed by what was happening, I got on the bed. Then Andrea hopped in.

Crash! The mattress fell through the bed frame. Andrea jumped up: "I'm not that heavy!" With that being her immediate reaction, she somehow endeared herself to me even more. I led her into the guest bedroom and we spent the night there.

In the morning, I made us breakfast and she went to her office.

My bed had no slats holding up the box spring – it rested on the bed rails. I'd never had a problem with it, but after Andrea left I drove to a neighborhood lumberyard and had them cut 1x4s to length. If two of us were going to be in the bed sometimes, it needed slats.

Through that week, Andrea and I spent more and more time together. She still went to her office to work or went out with other friends. I still went to my appointments and met friends for coffee. But the more time I spent with Andrea, the deeper in love I fell. So kind, so sweet, such a lovely person, she was easy for me to love. I had a much harder time accepting that she loved me – me, Kate, an old transgender woman who'd struggled all her life to find herself.

After Christmas, we went to Seattle together. We spent the

week exploring the city and just being happy together. It was a week of joy and, despite our ages, young love.

By the time we got back to Portland we were a couple. Yet Andrea continued to struggle. Her father had told her she needed to marry a man so he could take care of her. And all of society told her the same thing. She'd married men, but now she'd fallen in love with me, a transgender woman. She agonized over whether to follow her head and its scripting or to follow her heart. It was a dilemma I had worked through myself – whether to follow society's expectations or to be who I am. But how do you know who you are? How do you know your heart is true?

Andrea's struggles continued. We spent more and more time together, but then Andrea would say she needed to take a break. She'd say perhaps we shouldn't see each other for three or four days. Then later that same day, she would call, saying she needed to see me. It was hard for her. She was venturing into new territory, and it was scary for her. She'd married twice and twice made a mistake. She was wary, especially having fallen for this unusual creature that I am.

I was sympathetic to what she was going through. I knew from my own struggles that she had to work it out for herself. I could only support her and love her while I waited. To me, Andrea was a gift – a totally unexpected gift beyond measure. I would happily accept whatever of this magical gift she was able to give me. Accept it, cherish it, and be grateful without reservation.

16

BEING ✳ 2012-

"It takes courage to grow up and become who you really are."
— e. e. cummings

Through the years, I never wanted my picture taken while cross-dressed. It was the age of film, and I'd have to take the film some-where to be developed and printed. I was in the military, with a security clearance. I didn't want a record of my activity.

But sometime in the 90s, while living in Maryland, Polly convinced me to let her take my picture. When the prints came back, she said: "See? You're not transformed." She got to the central issue.

I desired transformation, where I would no longer be him but her – or at least a better, softer, perhaps even prettier him. Even looking in the mirror, I could see this other me. But the photo-graph was of a man in women's clothes. How sad.

It was a reality check. I was disappointed that putting on a skirt didn't make me appear to be a woman – I looked like a man wearing a skirt. But I better understood that it takes more than clothes to make the woman. And wearing women's clothes for me was more about how it made me feel than how it made me look.

Twenty or more years later, I am legally female and able to live as a woman. But transformed? Yes and no.

It is easy to believe in fairy tales. Cinderella is discovered to be a beauty. The woman working the lunch counter is discovered as a cinematic star. The poor paperboy, through luck and hard work and inherent virtue becomes a wealthy, self-made man. The struggling single mother wins the lottery, which lifts her into a life of ease.

But we carry our upbringing and memories and past life with us.

I am now Kate. I live happily as a woman and am treated as one. I love it. But I have a male skeleton – wide chest and shoulders, narrow hips, long trunk, a skull more masculine than feminine. My voice was deepened by testosterone.

I was socialized male. Sometimes I find myself in social situations reacting, acting, saying things that are from that socialization. My experiences are those of a male. I never menstruated, never worried about being pregnant myself, never worried much about being raped. In my working life, people thought I was a man and gave me the benefits of that assessment.

I am a hybrid – more woman than man, but some of each. Perhaps it would be otherwise if I'd transitioned when I was 20 and lived most of my life as a woman instead of most of it as a man who never was a man.

Am I transformed? Not really. I carry too much of my past with me. Am I free to be who I am? Yes. And with that perhaps transformation isn't the central issue after all.

There are at least two aspects of my transition – physical and social. Physically, I love having breasts and no longer having that junk hanging off me. And the hormones have a different feel to them. Male and female sexuality is different, at least as much as

I've experienced it. Male sexuality is outward, thrusting, and centered on the groin. Female sexuality is inward, opening, and diffuse. It can permeate the whole body, the whole being. Men are the bee; women are the blossoming flower.

The social aspect of being a woman is for me much deeper, more satisfying, more complex. People treat men and women differently. Men tend to be protective, deferential, and/or dismissive toward women — sometimes all of these at the same time. Women tend to be less guarded and friendlier with other women. Men either ignore other men or nod to each other, like two warriors passing. Women tend to look in each other's eyes and give a little smile of greeting or understanding, like an acknowledgment of connection and each other's common experience. Men don't talk in the men's room; women chat with each other, whether they know each other or not.

Early on, I told Casey that I was worried about transitioning because I didn't know if I would be accepted into the club. Some months later, when the women's group at church in Laramie invited me to join them, she said: "Looks like you've been invited into the club." I laughed. Yes, I had literally been invited into the club. But it's still hard for me sometimes – I'd spent too long outside, looking in.

I never felt the collegiality of men, except perhaps in the military. Women have been very kind in accepting me as one of them. I feel like this is where I belong – where I've always belonged.

When I went to Casey's wedding as one of the mothers of the bride, a groomsman from out of town was confused. He was familiar with someone having two mothers, but one of them was now married to a man. What was going on? Casey reported to me that one of her girlfriends explained it: "Oh, Kate is Casey's father. She's just happier as a woman." Yes. Whatever I am, I am just happier as a woman.

Already we are in a different time. Talking about writing this story I told a woman I had just met that I am transgender and am writing a story about it for my daughter. This woman was happy I was writing about my struggle to be who I am. We all struggle, to a greater or lesser extent, to be who we are. This is certainly true, but my point in mentioning this interaction is that times have changed. I wouldn't have been comfortable revealing that aspect of me to a relative stranger 20 years ago. And that stranger probably wouldn't have the background knowledge and experience to respond the way she did.

Society's understanding of the wide variety of what it means to be human continues to grow. We aren't stamped out in a factory. We are living organisms, with the wonderful variety that occurs naturally. If only we will let it.

Sometimes I wonder what my life would have been like if I hadn't been born transgender. Would I have been a better student? Would I have married a man and had children? Would I have chosen well? Would I have later partnered with a woman? Would I, at age 70, have been satisfied with my life? There is no way to tell, of course.

And once in a while I find myself wondering how it would have worked out if I had transitioned before age 20, before my voice changed, before I got whiskers, before my shoulders and chest widened and my hips didn't. But that's harder to imagine, especially given the time I was that age. Would it even have been possible for me to transition in the 1950s or 60s, before the word transgender existed?

Perhaps tellingly, I never wonder what it would have been like to be born with my male body but not transgender. After all, that person wouldn't be me.

AFTERWORD

"Change nothing, just be yourself to experience bliss."
— Tapan Ghosh, *Faceless: The Only Way Out*

Through the spring of 2012, Andrea gradually moved in, bringing more of her belongings to my condo, living there with me. We mixed our dishes. We took down some of my pictures and hung hers. We were blending our belongings and our lives. In the summer her brother Tom helped us move the rest of her things to my condo. She wasn't ready to sell her own condo – she wanted to keep it as a fallback option – but more and more we were building a life together. That November, on election day, afraid the haters would get back in power, I took Andrea to the county building to register us as domestic partners while that option was still available.

And two years later, when it finally became legal for us, we were married at First Unitarian Church, where we'd met, with my daughter Casey and her husband, Valerie and her husband, Gretchen and her husband from Minneapolis, Andrea's brothers Tom and Paul, her cousin Linda from Bremerton, my Maryland friends Mark and Bob, and three dozen or so of our Portland friends in attendance. It was a truly magical day.

I must be the luckiest person alive.

～

In the dream I am surrounded, enclosed, confined. It keeps getting closer, tightening. I twitch, jerk, resist. I am scared but determined. I don't cry out. Not this time. Not yet. I begin to kick.

Andrea touches my shoulder. "Are you dreaming?" she asks. Awake now but still in the dream's grip, I say, "I hope so." She curls up to me and I hold her. Her fierce love pours into me, quieting me, healing me.

Do you have these dreams too, dear reader? Dreams where you are corralled, confined? Where they can control you, maybe hurt you, maybe kill you? Because of who you are? Because of how you were born?

Lying there with Andrea, I can feel her slipping back to sleep again. I remember the dream, but the warmth of her body next to mine, her steady breathing, they assure me: I am safe now. And I drift back to sleep, counting my blessings.

NOTES

6. Exploring ✳ 1983-1984

1. *Conundrum*, Jan Morris, 1974; *Mirror Image*, Nancy Hunt, 1978; *Second Serve – The Renée Richards Story*, Renée Richards with John Ames, 1983.
2. https://www.nytimes.com/2017/10/07/world/americas/brazil-transgender-pabllo-vittar.html?_r=0

10. Acknowledging ✳ 2008-2009

1. https://www.susans.org
2. https://www.washingtonpost.com/national/health-science/long-shadow-cast-by-psychiatrist-on-transgender-issues-finally-recedes-at-johns-hopkins/2017/04/05/e851e56e-0d85-11e7-ab07-07d9f521f6b5_story.html?utm_term=.dcf2047925ec

13. Venturing ✳ 2009-2010

1. *True Selves: Understanding Transsexualism – For Families, Friends, Coworkers, and Helping Professionals* by Mildred Brown and Chloe Ann Rounsley.

ACKNOWLEDGMENTS

My thanks go first to Melissa Madenski, who first read my story and said I had to finish it and tell it to a wider audience. I have to admit, Melissa, that there were times I wished you hadn't set me on this path, but in the end I know you were right. The telling has helped me come to terms with the difficult parts of the tale.

I thank my many other readers for their comments and encouragement: Kay Schmerber, Ruth Ross, my writing workshop leader Lê Thi Diem Thúy, Carol Bosworth, The Reverend Bill Sinkford, Mo & Lois Weathers, Jan Wainscott, Caroline and Don Lehman, and Bill Dickey.

I thank my editors Sarah Sentilles and Anna Paradox for their help toward telling the story in a more readable form.

I thank Eddie Passadore for his encouragement, and for his recognition that this story could be told in film. His work led to the movie *Strictly for the Birds*. That was a fun and unexpected experience that tells the story in a different medium and perhaps to a different audience.

I thank my daughter Casey Lalonde for her encouragement to

write stories for her, and I thank her for her loving appreciation of my efforts.

And with deep gratitude I thank my wife Andrea Drury for her loving encouragement, her excellent proofreading, and her steadfast support through the vicissitudes of pulling this sometimes painful story out of the barricaded recesses of my mind and into the light of the public eye.

With the efforts of all these people, may this telling help others to tell their stories, and through that telling, heal their hurts.

ABOUT THE AUTHOR

Born transgender decades before the word existed, Kate Birdsall struggled to make sense of it all. Through many relocations and many jobs, including a career in the Coast Guard, she grew to be able to claim herself at the age of 65, while living in Laramie, Wyoming.

Kate started writing for her daughter, and expanded her memoirs to show that not all transgender stories are tragedies. She hopes her life, in her autobiography and in the feature film *Strictly for the Birds*, will support others in their efforts to find their true selves.

Kate blogs at travelswithkate.com. Originally from Detroit, Kate lives in Portland with her wife Andrea.

Made in the USA
Las Vegas, NV
14 April 2022

47494474R00116